Building Cabinet Doors & Drawers

Building Cabinet Doors & Drawers

BY DANNY PROULX

STOBART DAVIES

HERTFORD

BUILDING CABINET DOORS & DRAWERS

by

Danny Proulx

© 2000 by Danny Proulx

Reprinted 2002

ISBN 0-85442-089-4

Printed in the United States of America
23456789

British Library Cataloging in Publication Data
A catalogue record for this book is available from the British Library

Published by
Stobart Davies Ltd., Priory House, Priory Street, Hertford SG14 1RN

Building Cabinet Doors & Drawers

CONTENTS

Introduction ....*Page 7*

Working Safe at Woodworking...*Page 8*

Chapter 1 **Joinery Overview**...*Page 10*

Chapter 2 **Exploring Door Options** ....*Page 22*

Chapter 3 **Building Drawers & Pull-Outs**......................................*Page 34*

Chapter 4 **Making Slab Doors** ....*Page 48*

Chapter 5 **Frame-and Flat-Panel Doors**..*Page 58*

Chapter 6 **Frame-and Raised-Panel Doors**....................................*Page 74*

Chapter 7 **Multi-Panel Cope-and-Stick Doors** ....*Page 82*

Chapter 8 **Glass Cabinet Doors**...*Page 84*

Chapter 9 **Tongue-and-groove Doors**...*Page 92*

Chapter 10 **Making Tambour Doors** ....*Page 96*

Chapter 11 **Installing Pocket Doors**...*Page 100*

Chapter 12 **Installing Doors & Drawer Fronts**............................*Page 106*

Index ....*Page 111*

ACKNOWLEDGMENTS

A technical writer needs a lot of support. Mastering all the disciplines that are needed to put a woodworking book together is not possible. Design, concept, writing, graphics, construction and photography all require very demanding skills.

I am very fortunate to have a great team. To my wife, Gale, my woodworking assistant, Jack Chaters, and my photographic expert, Michael Bowie, thank you very much for the support.

STEP-BY-STEP PHOTOGRAPHY:

Danny Proulx

COVER AND LAB WORK:

Michael Bowie

Lux Photographic

95A Beech St.

Suite 204

Ottawa, Ont.

K1S 3J7

Canada

WORKSHOP:

Rideau Cabinets

P.O. Box 331

Russell, Ont.

K4R 1E1

Canada

ABOUT THE AUTHOR

Danny Proulx is the owner of Rideau Cabinets and is a contributing editor for *CabinetMaker Magazine*. He also contributes freelance articles to *Canadian Home Workshop, Popular Woodworking* and other magazines. He is the author of *Build Your Own Kitchen Cabinets, The Kitchen Cabinetmaker's Building and Business Manual, How to Build Classic Garden Furniture* and *Smart Shelving and Storage Solutions.*

Danny can be reached through the Rideau Cabinets website at www.cabinetmaking.com

TECHNICAL SUPPORT

The following companies have been a tremendous help in creating this book:

Julius Blum Inc.

1-800-438-6788

http://www.blum.com

Delta International Machinery Corp.

1-800-438-2486

http://www.deltawoodworking.com

L.R.H Enterprises Inc.

1-800-423-2544

http://www.lrhent.com

Rout-R-Slide

Jessem Tool Co.

1-800-436-6799

http://www.jessem.com

Ryobi Canada Inc.

1-800-265-6778

http://www.ryobi.com

Tenryu America Inc.

1-800-951-7297

http://www.tenryu.com

Wolfcraft Inc.

1-630-773-4777

http://www.wolfcraft.com

INTRODUCTION

This book has been written in response to the many questions I have received from hundreds of cabinet-making enthusiasts asking me about building their own doors for kitchen, entertainment and other cabinet projects.

The Complete Project

My earlier books, as well as many others I've seen, have detailed building plans for all sorts of cabinets. However, the process of building doors has not been fully explained. In many instances, instructions for all the possible door styles for each project would fill dozens of pages. That's what I hope to accomplish in this book, making it a companion manual for your favorite woodworking books. There are dozens of options offered so you should be able to find a door style to match any cabinet.

I'll show you how to build all types of door styles— from simple and basic to fancy and involved. There is a chapter on joinery which, when mastered, will allow you to build any door you need for your projects.

If you are planning to build new kitchen cabinets for your home, building your own doors will save you money. Doors are among the most expensive items in any kitchen renovation, so being able to build your own will be a real plus.

And, if you are going to tackle that kitchen cabinet-making project, there's a chapter on building drawers. Like doors, they can be a major cost consideration and the process of drawer building can be intimidating to many woodworkers. I'll show you how to build drawers successfully, easily and inexpensively.

I will also explore many of the new man-made wood products available, including particleboard (PB) sheets that have paper and epoxy coatings (referred to as melamine) as well as PB sheets that have real wood veneers attached. These open up a wealth of possibilities in door- and drawer-making.

Some woodworking purists don't believe in using these composite boards. But I would advise you not to sell these modern products short. They are stable, inexpensive and they do conserve our woodland resources. I have built hundreds of cabinets using PB with decorative moldings and they've turned out great.

A door- and drawer-making book wouldn't be complete without an in-depth look at mounting hardware, both the traditional North American hardware and the European version that has made mounting doors and drawers a snap. I will describe all the possibilities for your projects.

Door- and drawer-building can be fun and satisfying. Take your time, explore all the options, then build some of these great door and drawer styles for your own projects.

WORKING SAFE AT WOODWORKING

SAFETY EQUIPMENT

Working with tools can sometimes be dangerous. Over the last thirty years, I've had my share of nicks, scrapes, and one serious accident.

When I look back on all the times I've had a "close call," I realize they were caused by a number of things. Primarily, I wasn't paying full attention to the task at hand. But there were a few times that I was tired and should not have been in the shop. Often, we don't take the time to read all the safety instructions packaged with a new tool.

To avoid injury, read all the manufacturer's information, don't work if you're tired, and eliminate any distractions so you can fully focus on the task. Spending the afternoon in a hospital emergency ward isn't much fun.

Hearing protection, safety glasses and dust masks are a necessity in the workshop.

Protecting Yourself

Sawdust is a fact of life in the shop and it can be dangerous. Wear a dust mask when sanding or with any operation that creates dust.

Your ability to hear is another one of the senses that can be affected when using power tools. Wear earplugs or any of the other hearing protection aids that are available. Never turn on a machine without wearing hearing protection.

When you start woodworking, the first thing you should do is put on your safety glasses. If you normally wear glasses, get a prescription pair that is safety-rated.

Always know where your hands are when operating equipment. I ask myself that question each time I turn on a tool. And always use push sticks, paddles and guards.

In this book, you'll see some of the equipment operating without a guard. That is only being done for photographic clarity. All machines should be operated with all safety attachments in place at all times.

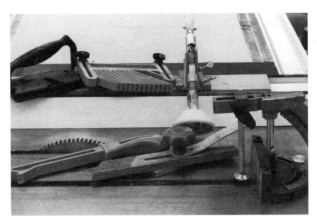

Push sticks, paddles, feather boards and other equipment such as anti-kickback devices should be used at all times.

SAFETY RULES

Here are just a few safety rules that should be kept in mind and taught to anyone who works in your woodshop.

Tool Safety

The router is one of the woodworker's most important tools. It can create designs in minutes that would have taken a person days to finish by hand. It's one of the best tools a woodworker has but it demands lots of respect.

Be mindful of where your hands are with this and other power tools. High-speed router and drill bits, saw blades and sanding belts can just as easily cut you as wood. Be careful!

1. Read and understand all the instructions that come with your tools.

2. Always wear safety glasses because even the most innocent looking hand tool is a potential hazard.

3. Be aware of the position of your hands and fingers when operating power tools.

4. Keep a fire extinguisher in the woodshop and have it inspected regularly.

5. Install a smoke alarm in the shop, as there is always a potential combustion hazard with sawdust and chemicals.

6. Wear hearing protection when using machines or power tools.

7. Use caution when handling or disposing of chemicals.

8. Wear a dust mask or respirator when there is a potential of high dust or chemical odor.

9. Work under proper lighting. If the area is properly lit, the chance of an accident is greatly decreased.

10. Never attempt to change blades or bits on a tool that's connected to power. Pull the plug or turn off the circuit breaker.

11. Do not work when you are tired or taking medication.

12. Keep blades and bits sharp. Dull tools can cause an accident.

These are a few safety rules that everyone should follow. But above all else, use common sense. If an operation seems dangerous—DO NOT DO IT! Find another way to safely accomplish the task.

Chapter 1   JOINERY OVERVIEW

DOOR AND DRAWER JOINERY

There are a number of different joints we'll use to build the doors and drawers covered in this book. They include butt, miter, lap, rabbet, groove, dado, mortise-and-tenon, dovetail and box joints. You may think these joints have strange-sounding names and may think they appear difficult to make, but when you get down to the basics of each, you will discover that they are actually quite simple to build with a few tools.

All of these joints can be made by hand. Before we had electricity and power tools, all joinery was hand-made, using chisels, saws and planes. Power tools have made the process much easier, and some of the jigs on the market further simplify the process.

What is the best joint and which do we use? There isn't a "best" joint. Each has its own application and the choice depends on many things such as stress, materials being used and visual appearance. These will determine which joint is best suited for each application.

Types of Stress

Shear, racking, compression and tension are all forms of stress that act on joints. Some act to a greater degree depending on the application, so it is wise to be aware of the forces affecting your joinery.

Shear is force applied to a joint, trying to slide it apart. For example, the butt joint used to join boards at right angles, such as those in a bookcase, has weight applied causing a downward or shearing pressure.

Racking is a twisting force common to doors, drawers and cabinetry. The force applied can throw doors and cabinets out of square, causing binding and joint failure.

Compression stress pushes the joint together, and tension tries to pull the joint apart. All joints are affected by one or more of these forces.

Wood Movement

Wood is an organic material. It will expand and contract even after the tree it came from has been cut, milled and dried. Varying humidity levels during seasonal changes cause the wood cells to absorb and give off moisture, which results in wood movement.

In many instances, joints are fashioned by attaching wood pieces at an angle. Movement in the wood acts on each piece at an uneven rate because the grain direction and pattern of each is different. An example of dealing with movement is with the raised panel in a frame-and-panel door—the panel is left to "float" in the door frame with a little extra space, so that expansion won't spread the stile and rail joints apart.

Adhesives and Fasteners

Yellow carpenter's glue, an aliphatic-resin-based liquid, is a general-purpose woodworking glue suitable for just about all joinery. If any of your projects are to be used outside, you may be better off using the relatively new family of water-resistant one-part polyurethane glues, however.

Many types of fasteners will be used when building drawers and doors. Dowels and biscuits are reinforcement fastening aids, which, along with the glue, can measurably improve the strength of a joint. And mechanical fasteners, like screws and nails, are often used to secure the joint until the adhesive sets up.

One of the newest fasteners is the particleboard (PB) or chipboard screw. It should be the only screw used when joining PB material. The shaft of this screw is thin and the threads are coarse. Some chipboard screws have nibs under the head to lock the screw in place. But remember—always drill a pilot hole before installing these screws. The hole allows the screw to cut a thread, instead of wedging and splitting the board.

Butt Joints

The butt joint is simple to put together because it requires nothing except two straight-cut boards. Its strength depends on the glue and on the mechanical fasteners used to secure the boards.

Butt joints are often reinforced with biscuits, splines or dowels. However, most glued-up raised panels used for doors are simply edge-glued, and the builder relies on properly surfaced edges to maximize board contact.

Another common application for the butt joint is drawer-making. Wood drawers have glued and nailed joints, while PB drawers depend entirely on screwed butt joints.

To maximize the effectiveness of a butt joint, be certain both boards are cut straight and square. A good edge is achieved with an accurate saw or, in the case of panels, a well-tuned jointer.

The butt joint can be used to join boards edge-to-edge, end-to-face, edge-to-face and so on. Orientation of the grain, common when creating panels, is important to stabilize the joint. Most woodworkers alternate the growth ring patterns so that the cupping and warping of one board will counteract the one beside it.

Butt joints are often used when building PB drawers. The strength of this joint depends entirely on the chipboard screw.

The particleboard or chipboard screw should be used when joining PB materials.

Dowels and Biscuits

Dowels have long been in use to strengthen many different types of joints. Biscuits, which are relatively new to woodworkers, are quickly becoming the preferred method of joint reinforcement.

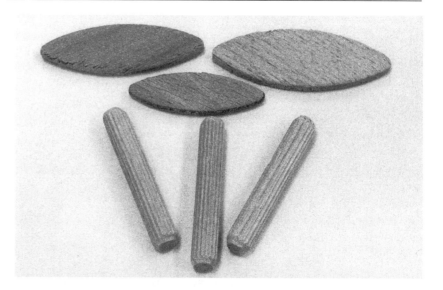

You'll often hear the term "biscuit joinery" when the proper name is "plate joinery." However, the term "biscuit" has caught on so that usually only manufacturers now refer to the tool as a plate joiner.

The process could be called by any name and I would still continue to believe biscuit joinery is one of the best inventions in woodworking. Installing biscuits is much easier than aligning holes for dowels. In fact, once the plate joiner is adjusted, alignment is automatic.

A plate joiner is a great addition to any woodworking shop.

Plate joinery involves cutting semi-circular slots in both boards to be joined. Glue is applied to the edges of each board and in the slots. An oval-shaped beech wood biscuit is put in the slots on one board and the boards are clamped. Biscuits increase the gluing surface and that is beneficial in achieving a stronger joint. But, more importantly, the beech wood ovals swell when they absorb the moisture in the glue and increase the strength of the joint even further.

Each board to be joined is marked, so that slots can be cut with a plate joiner. The beech wood biscuits are inserted into the slots on one of the boards after glue has been applied. The boards are then clamped together.

Spline Joinery

Splines are often used to rein-force butt joints. Both boards must be grooved or dadoed. Then a thin strip of wood is inserted into the grooves.

This is a good way to dramatically improve the strength of a butt joint. Much like biscuit joinery, the spline increases the gluing surface and mechanically locks the joint.

To make this joint, be certain you first have a good fit between the two boards being joined. Then cut a dado or a groove in each board. Next, cut a spline to fit snugly in the grooves.

Apply glue to the joint surfaces, including the grooves. Insert the spline, then clamp the joint together until the glue dries.

Cut grooves or dadoes in each board.

Cut a spline that fits tightly in the grooves. Apply glue to all surfaces and clamp the joint.

Miter Joints

Miter joints are a form of butt joint but, because each piece of wood is cut at an angle, the available glue surface is increased. Therefore, the miter joint is stronger than the simple butt joint.

Miter joints are widely used in the carpentry and cabinetmaking industries. The joint is popular because it is pleasing to look at and it hides the end grain of each board.

These joints will be used a great deal when building doors and drawers and, for the most part, are relatively simple to make. Two boards are joined at an angle. In almost all cases, the angle of each board is one-half the joint angle.

For example, a 90-degree miter needs two pieces of wood each cut at 45 degrees to properly form the joint. A 30-degree miter requires two boards with 15-degree cuts, and so on.

Miter joinery gets its strength from two closely fitted glued surfaces. However, mechanical fasteners such as splines and biscuits can strengthen the joint.

Accurate cutting of each piece of the joint is essential in creating a good miter joint.

The biscuit is a good way to increase the quality of any miter joint. A mini-plate-joiner is an ideal tool for anyone making a large number of miters.

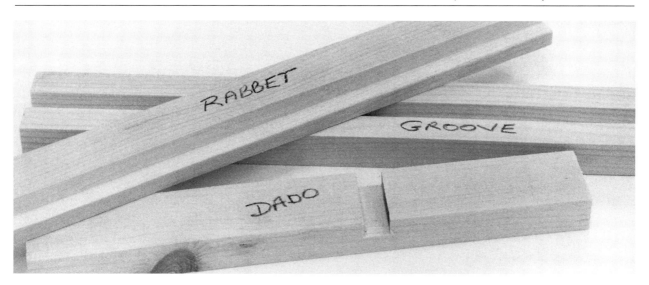

Dado, Groove and Rabbet Joints

These joints are all related and are all made the same way. The position of the cut on a board determines its name. A dado is cut across the grain, a groove is cut with the grain and a rabbet is cut on the edge of a board.

Joints such as these, utilizing a channel cut into the wood, are easily made with a router or a table saw. They are probably the most commonly used joints in the cabinetmaking industry, are mechanically strong and are easily made. They can be used in many different situations, which is why they are so popular.

Two rabbet cuts form a corner half-lap joint.

A dado joint for right-angle joinery is an excellent method of supporting shelves.

A double dado is a mechanically sound joint when building drawers.

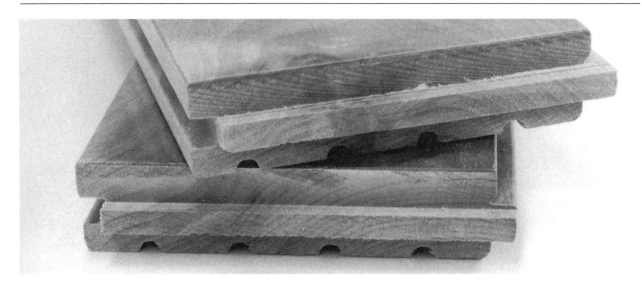

Tongue-and-Groove Joints

The tongue-and-groove joint is quite often the joint of choice for many door styles. A raised-panel door has a groove cut in the rails and stiles and a tongue on the raised panel.

The closed groove or "track" formed by joining stiles and rails allows the panel to float in the frame. It is not necessary to mechanically bond the panel because it is supported on all sides.

Solid-core raised-panel doors are often constructed using a form of tongue-and-groove that is commonly called a cope-and-stick joint.

Cut the groove on a table saw.

The tongue can also be easily formed on the table saw.

Mortise-and-Tenon Joints

This is one of the woodworker's favorite joints. It has been used for centuries to attach wood, and continues to be commonly used by all woodworkers.

The mortise—or hole—part of the joint can be cut on a drill press, or with a dedicated mortise press. Holes can be left rounded at the corners, or chiseled square. It is your decision—each method is equally strong.

A drill press is the ideal tool for forming the mortise because the hole will be straight. Hand-drilling, although an option, is not recommended if you want perfect mortises.

If you plan to use the mortise-and-tenon as one of your regular joints, a tenoning jig for the table saw is a good investment. The tenon is accurately cut square and perfectly proportioned with one of these jigs.

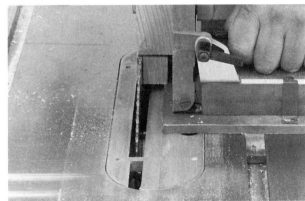

The tenon is easily cut with a table saw and dado blade, or with a tenon jig.

Cut the mortise using a drill press and Forstner bit.

Leaving the mortise with round corners means you'll need to round over the tenon corners with a wood rasp.

Box, or Finger, Joints

Box joints are simple, decorative and mechanically strong because of all the extra gluing surfaces on the fingers.

Fit the table saw with a wood fence that has a finger attached. The finger should equal the width of the space you are cutting.

Remember, start one end of each board with a finger and the other with a space. You will get perfect box joints every time.

Use a table saw or router table. But, remember to custom-make the fence with a pin equal to the width of the box joint.

That pin is spaced one pin's thickness away from the blade. The first board cut is made with the board tight against the jig pin. Afterward, set the hole cut on the pin and begin cutting fingers the entire width of the board. The second pass begins cutting spaced one pin width away from the jig pin.

Dry-fit the joint. If it's a little tight, use a wood rasp to gently widen the holes. Once the joint is perfect, apply glue and clamp the joint.

Cutting box joints on a table saw is easy with a shop-made jig.

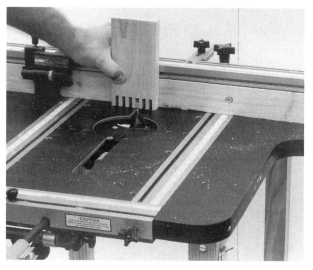

If you own a router table, such as this Rout-R-Slide by Jessem, you can push the bit into the small workpiece.

DOVETAIL JOINTS

The dovetail joint, with all its variations, is the most challenging joint to make, but it is also one of the strongest and finest of the furniture joints. Like the box joint, it has been a standard for centuries.

Making Dovetail Joints with a Jig

There are many dovetail jigs on the market today. A good high-quality jig is relatively expensive, but it will last you a lifetime. If you make many dovetail joints, a good jig is well worth the money.

Look at the different systems on the market. Look at how the metal is machined and see what accessories are available. A poor jig will only make a poor joint.

The high-quality jigs will have a well-written manual that is worth reading thoroughly. Follow the manufacturer's instructions and practice making the joint.

Use a carbide dovetail bit in your router and make certain it is sharp. The quality of the dovetail joint depends largely on clean, accurately cut pins and tails.

You can hand-cut the dovetail joint or use a jig. It is a matter of personal preference. Whichever method you choose, try to master this joint because it adds a lot to the quality and visual appearance of any project.

You will need a router and high-quality dovetail bit to cut well-fitting dovetail joints.

Hand-Cut Dovetails

Step 1-Scribe the pin depth with a marking gauge on the outside face of the board. The depth is equal to the thickness of the board.

Step 2-Mark the pins with a 10-degree angle. Divide them up equally across the board end for spacing and width.

Step 3-Cut the dovetail pins on the waste side of the pencil line, leaving the pencil line showing as you cut. Use a backsaw (tenon saw) or a Japanese pull-saw.

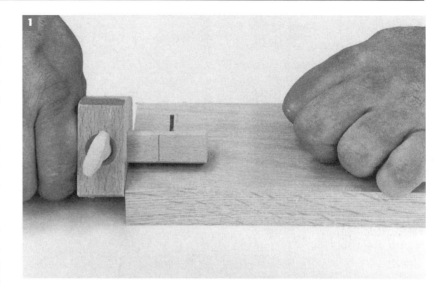

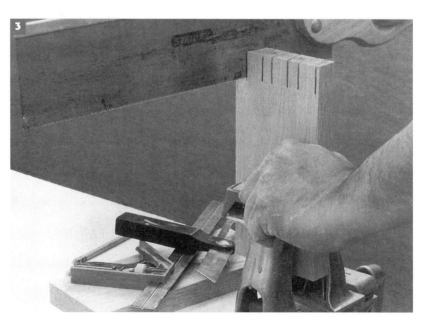

Step 4-Remove the waste using a coping saw to angle down from the top corner to the opposite bottom corner with your first cut. Remove the balance of the waste with a straight cut.

Step 5-Mark the tails using the pin board as a guide. Cut and remove the waste from around the tails.

Step 6-Dry-fit the joint before gluing. Use a wood file to true-up the pins and tails until you achieve a nice, tight-fitting joint.

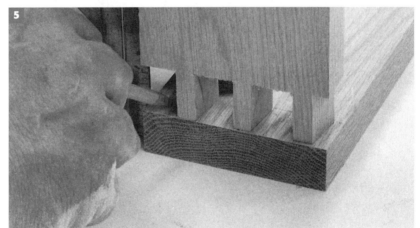

Chapter 2   EXPLORING DOOR OPTIONS

MOUNTING STYLES

There are many types and styles of cabinet doors. And there are just as many different ways to hinge the doors to the cabinets.

Two of the most common mounting styles are the overlay and the inset. The overlay door is attached to the cabinet or carcass box with hinges and partially covers the front edges of the cabinet. The inset door is set into the cabinet opening, flush with the outside face. There isn't a "better" or "best" style—one mounting style is as good as the other. Your choice will be based on your personal preference and on matching the cabinet design that you are building.

There are, of course, variables on these two, including half-overlay and pocket-mounting styles. However, the two generally accepted terms for door-fitting styles are the overlay and the inset door.

Door Anatomy

Doors made from one piece of material—whether it's particleboard or solid wood—are called slab doors.

Those made of multiple parts are known as frame-and-panel doors. They are also referred to as board-and-batten or tongue-and-groove. It all depends on construction style. There are also door-making styles whose names are taken from particular builders—the Shaker-style door, for instance.

Nevertheless, a door made from a number of parts has two "stiles," or vertical members, and two horizontal pieces called "rails." The fifth piece is the center panel, which can either be solid wood or plywood veneer. There are a few exceptions to this terminology and we'll examine all the variables in upcoming chapters.

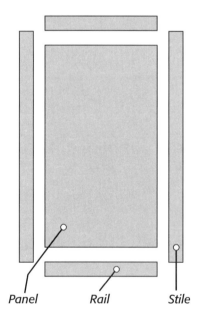

Panel   *Rail*   *Stile*

DOOR-MOUNTING HARDWARE

There are many different hardware options available for hanging a cabinet door. The traditional North American cabinet hinge, which has long been a standard, is available in dozens of styles and finishes.

European Hinges

In the last few years, door-mounting hardware from Europe has become a very popular alternative to the North American variety. The "Euro hidden hinge" is now widely used as standard kitchen cabinet door hardware.

The hidden hinge usually requires a hole drilled in the door. That task may seem a bit challenging to some people but it is actually a straightforward process.

There are a few things to learn when working with the hidden hinge. For instance, these hinges are classified with terms such as full overlay, half-overlay and inset. Overlay simply refers to the amount of cabinet, if any, that is covered by the door.

Parts of a Hinge

The hidden hinge comes in two parts: the hinge, or "boss," which is mounted on the door, and the "mounting plate," which is attached to the cabinet side.

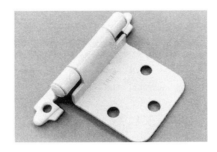

The boss is attached to the mounting plate with a screw or a clip pin. The clip-on method is becoming very popular because it allows the door to be removed from the mounting plate without disturbing any adjustments.

Degrees of Operation

Hidden hinges are also classed in terms of "degrees of opening." For standard door applications, the 100- to 120-degree opening hinge is common. But you can purchase hinges that will allow the door to open from 90 to 170 degrees. The term simply refers to the number of degrees of swing that the door can open from its closed position.

There are many traditional North American hinges available.

The European hidden hinge is one of the most widely used door hinges on the market today.

Adjusting doors with the European hidden hinge.

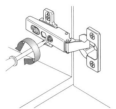

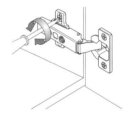

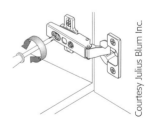

Courtesy Julius Blum Inc.

The clip-on hinge has become very popular.

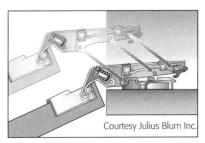

Courtesy Julius Blum Inc.

Hinge Applications

Degrees of opening; full-overlay, half-overlay or inset mounting; and mounting styles are varied. There are hinges for bi-fold doors often used in right-angled corner base cabinets in the kitchen cabinetmaking industry; slim-line hinges for glass door applications; and other specialty hinges to meet just about every need imaginable.

The majority of your applications will use a 95- to 110-degree opening hinge in the full overlay or inset style. However, there are times when you may want the door swinging completely open and out of the way. In that situation, a 170-degree hinge will be needed.

Mounting the Hinges

There are door-mounting jigs available at all woodworking stores. If you plan to use the hidden hinge for many of your projects, these jigs are worth buying.

If you're only using the hidden hinge occasionally, this quick and easy installation method does not require a jig.

This method works with all hinge-mounting applications, but it's based on using a 95- to 120-degree standard opening hinge. If you plan on installing a non-standard hinge, such as the 170-degree model, install the door with a standard hinge boss mounted in the door, then replace the hinge boss with a 170-degree boss after the door has been hung.

Step 1-Drill the 35mm holes in the door and mount the hinge boss.

Step 2-Secure the hinge boss in the hole. Use a square to position it 90 degrees to the door edge.

Step 3-Attach the mounting plate to the hinge boss.

Step 4-Place the door on the cabinet in its 90-degree open position. A 3/16-inch-thick spacer between the door edge and the cabinet side edge sets the correct door gap. Insert screws through the mounting plate to secure them to the cabinet side.

Step 5-Remove the door by releasing the hinge boss from the mounting plates. Insert the remaining screws to secure the mounting plates.

This door installation method will align the door in its proper position. Only minor adjustments will be needed to ensure a door perfectly installed on hidden hinges.

If you plan to use a 170-degree hinge, replace the boss and install the door on the same mounting plates. The wider-opening hinge will also be correctly positioned.

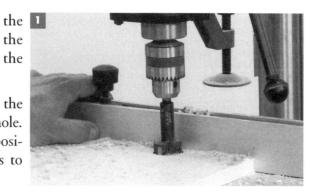

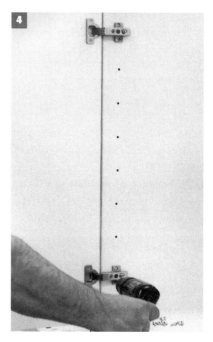

Full overlay, half- or twin overlay, and inset hinge set-ups.
Hinge dimensions and gap calculation based on factory setting (mounting plate spacing = 0mm).
Hinge and door protrusion at full opening angle.

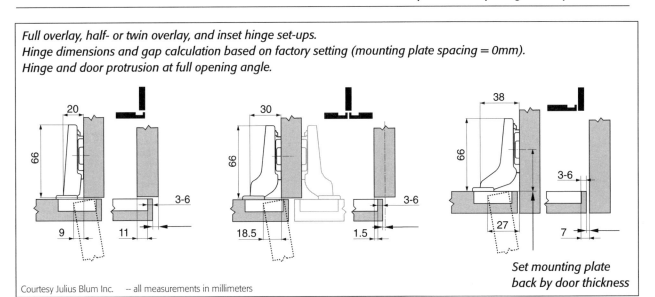

Set mounting plate
back by door thickness

Courtesy Julius Blum Inc.   -- all measurements in millimeters

Typical bi-fold and 170-degree hinges on cabinet doors. These two hinges are used together quite often, in a right-angle-corner base cabinet with a lazy Susan, for example.
Hinge dimensions and gap calculation based on factory setting (mounting plate spacing = 0mm).

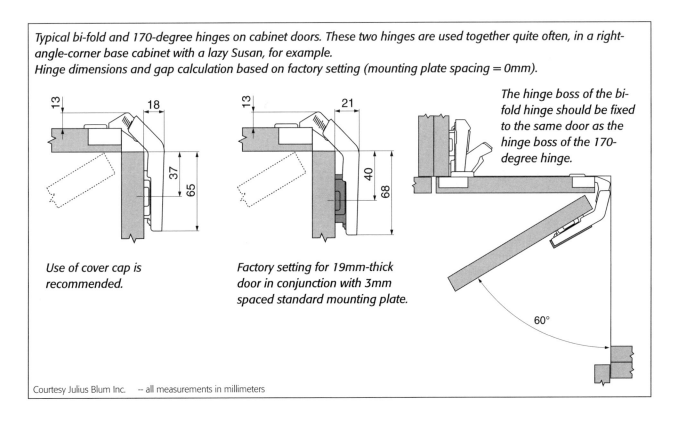

The hinge boss of the bi-fold hinge should be fixed to the same door as the hinge boss of the 170-degree hinge.

Use of cover cap is recommended.

Factory setting for 19mm-thick door in conjunction with 3mm spaced standard mounting plate.

Courtesy Julius Blum Inc.   -- all measurements in millimeters

The Full Overlay Hinge

This hinge covers the cabinet side by almost 5/8-inch when the door is closed. That overlay distance is largely based on frameless European-style kitchen cabinetry made with 16mm (5/8-inch) melamine-coated particleboard.

Two 35mm-diameter holes are drilled in the door to accept the hinge. The holes are set back about 1/8 inch from the edge of the door. Most hinge manufacturers, including Blum, whose products I use, require this set-up. However, check the specifications supplied by the manufacturer of the hinges you prefer.

The depth of the hinge hole depends upon the hinge being used. While there are slight variances, most hinges will fit in a hole 1/2 inch deep. Again, check the specifications of the hinge you plan to use.

The ideal bit for drilling a hinge hole is flat-bottomed, and often called a Forstner bit or a hinge-boring bit. I suggest you use a carbide-tipped hinge-boring bit because the binding adhesives used to manufacture particle core and plywood sheet goods are hard. High-speed steel bits will burn very quickly when drilling these boards.

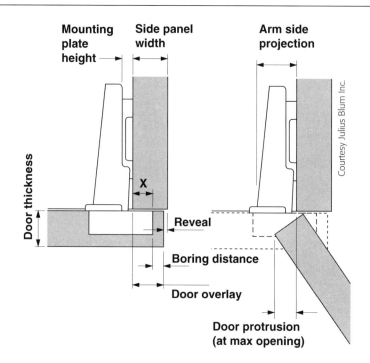

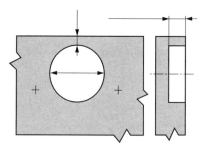

A 35mm hole for the full overlay hinge is set back 1/8 inch from the edge of the door.

The Half-Overlay Hinge

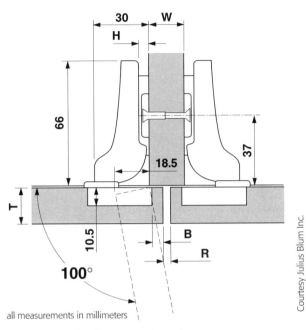

all measurements in millimeters

The half-overlay hinge overlaps the cabinet side by about 5/16 inch.

This hidden hinge is identical to the full overlay model with one slight difference.

It mounts on the door in the same way, but the overlap on the cabinet is only about 5/16 inch, or one-half the distance of the full overlay.

Manufacturers call this type a half-overlay hinge, but you might also see it called a twin or dual application hinge.

This hinge is used when two doors meet on one cabinet. This situation may arise when you have a series of doors side by side in a run, and the center doors meet on one cabinet. It is a limited-use hinge but there are times when the smaller overlay is needed.

The Inset Hinge

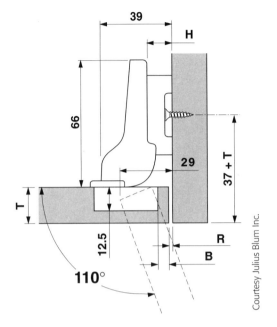

The inset hinge mounts the door flush with the face of the cabinet.

The inset hinge is perfect for flush-mounted doors. The mechanical ability of this hinge to maintain its position is an important feature and, unlike some of the earlier inset hinges and the traditional North American styles, this hinge is adjustable.

Building inset doors for any wood-working project is challenging. The cabinet opening must be square and the door has to be built with very close tolerances. Often, the clearance between the door and cabinet opening is 1/16 inch or less. A high-quality hinge is necessary for this application.

Study the specifications of the hinge you plan to use before building your inset doors. There are slight mounting differences depending on the manufacturer, and you should be aware of these before the doors are built.

Hinge Terminology and Dimensions

Hidden hinges are easy to install and you will soon appreciate all their benefits. The illustration below details some of the important dimensions and terminology associated with this hardware.

Study this illustration to become familiar with hidden-hinge terminology. It gives you some of the important dimensions you'll need when installing these hinges.

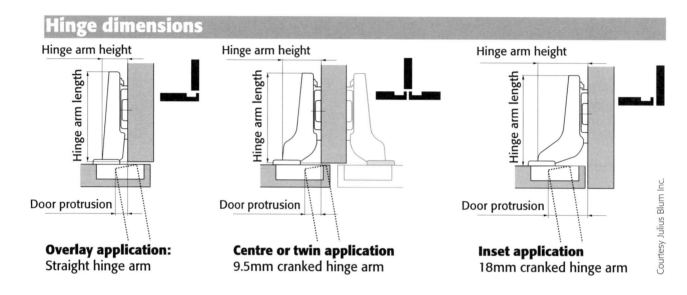

Courtesy Julius Blum Inc.

Overlay application:
Straight hinge arm

Centre or twin application
9.5mm cranked hinge arm

Inset application
18mm cranked hinge arm

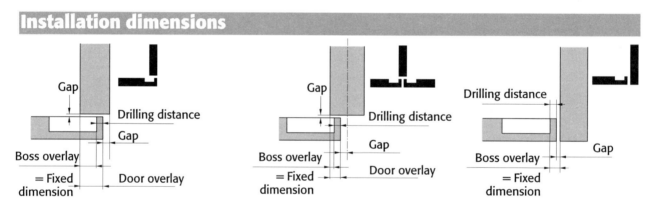

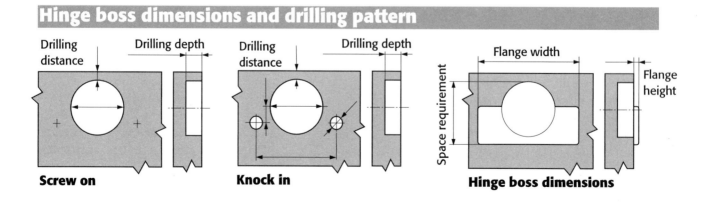

Screw on

Knock in

Hinge boss dimensions

HANDLE OPTIONS

There is not a great deal I can say about door handles. They are a necessity for most doors and choosing one is sometimes difficult because of the many styles available.

The cabinet style will often dictate which handle is most suitable—a modern nickel handle isn't appropriate for a Shaker-style cabinet, for instance. But the choice is not always that simple. Some suppliers, like mine, have more than two hundred different types of handles in stock.

Handles are mounted to the doors with machine screws. Manufacturers often include the screws with the handles, but most of those screws are for a standard 3/4-inch-thick door. You may have to run to the hardware store for different ones if your door isn't the so-called "standard" thickness. It's one minor annoyance that you may encounter when you are in a hurry to complete a project, so consider it ahead of time.

Door handles are installed on almost every door we build. There are hundreds of styles on the market.

Mounting Styles

Handles are attached with one or two screws through the back side of a door. The screw spacing isn't the same for every handle from each manufacturer. You will see 3-inch, 3-1/2 inch and 96mm on-center spacing plus a few more. It is not an important consideration, but it can be limiting if you need to change handles later.

What is the best position on the door to mount the handles? I don't believe there is a definite "best" position. I've seen handles 2 inches from the top, in the center of the door, on the edge of the door and in dozens of other positions. It's really a matter of looks and of personal choice. Sometimes the cabinet style that you're copying will provide the answer.

Function

My main concern with any handle is its ease of use. Is the door easy to operate? Will the handle be strong enough to stand up to the abuse when a cabinet is opened and closed a lot? Is the handle dangerous? Could a child's fingers get caught in the opening?

Older people, and those with diminished flexibility in their hands, sometimes have a hard time grasping door handles. If that situation applies in your house, you may want to consider a different handle style. Having everyone try a few samples, before you commit to purchasing all the hardware, is often well worth the effort. Unless money is not an issue, you will have to live with your choice for quite some time—and handles can be an expensive hardware item.

OTHER DOOR OPTIONS

This book will cover many door styles. All of them can be easily constructed in the home workshop. However, a few types are beyond the ability of the woodworker, particularly thermoplastic doors.

These doors are made with medium-density fiberboard (MDF) that has a pattern routed on the surface. The inlay patterns are created with a computer-controlled router. The designs are cut to simulate a raised-panel door style.

The MDF is then covered with a heat-shrunk plastic film on a high-pressure vacuum press. The plastic is forced into the pattern and takes on the contours of the design.

The latest styles of thermoplastic doors come in a range of colors. A few manufacturers are offering these doors with a texture that simulates wood grain.

Glass and Plastic Doors

Obviously, glass and Plexiglas door-making must also be left to the experts, but you may need one or two of these doors for a special cabinet. You will need to know what size to order—and here is where information about the hidden hinge is useful.

Determining Door Size

If you plan to install the standard 100-degree, full overlay hidden hinge, there is an easy rule-of-thumb used to determine door size.

First, the height is not critical. The door should overlay the cabinet at the top and bottom of the door by at least 1/4 inch.

The width of the door is critical. To calculate door width, measure the inside opening of the cabinet. Then, add 1 inch to that dimension to find the door size.

For example, a utility cabinet that has a 21-inch inside opening measurement will need one 22-inch-wide door or two 11-inch-wide doors. It's that simple. You will have to adjust the hinges slightly to get the correct gap between doors but, as you'll discover, this simple rule works in almost all cases.

Thermoplastic doors are becoming a popular choice for bathroom and Euro-style cabinets.

FACE-FRAME VS FRAMELESS CABINETRY

One other question you should consider, before building cabinet doors and ordering your hardware, is the cabinet style.

There are two main styles of cabinets, with many variations within each style, but being aware of the two main styles will help you decide on the door and the hardware required.

The basic face-frame cabinet has a hardwood face applied to the carcass.

Installing the face frame flush with the inside face of the cabinet's side board is another common building practice.

Face-Frame Cabinetry

This cabinet-building style consists of a simple cabinet box (carcass) and an applied hardwood frame on the front face. The carcass can be made of sheet materials such as plywood or particleboard. In early cabinets, you might see solid wood panels that have been glued together.

In some instances, the inside dimension of the face frame is less than the inside carcass dimension. The cabinet's side board is set back from the inside edge of the face-frame stiles (vertical members).

If that is the type of face-frame cabinet you are building, or if you have one that needs new doors, you can use traditional North American-style hinges or else hidden hinges with a face-frame mounting plate. Either hinge will work fine.

In the last few years, cabinetmakers—particularly in the kitchen cabinetmaking industry—have installed their face frames so that the inside edges of the face-frame stiles are flush with the inside faces of the cabinet.

Hardware Questions to Consider in Face-frame Cabinetry

Mounting doors with traditional North American-style hinges is easy with face-frame cabinets. There is usually ample room to mount the hinge on the face of the exterior frame.

Installing European hidden hinges on face-frame cabinets can present a few difficulties, but European hardware manufacturers have solved almost all of these problems with some unique hardware.

If the face frame has been installed so that its inside edges are flush with the inside surface of the cabinet carcass, install the hinges in the normal manner.

On the other hand, if the face frame has a smaller inside dimension than the carcass, a face-frame mounting plate must be used to mount the hidden hinge. It isn't a serious problem but it is one you should consider when ordering hinge hardware.

North American traditional hinges are simple to install on face-frame cabinets.

A European hidden hinge installed on a face-frame mounting plate.

Frameless Cabinetry

Cabinets built without a face frame are often referred to as "frameless" or "European" cabinets. The cabinet box does not have a wooden face frame applied to it. In almost all cases, the front edges of the cabinet box are covered with an iron-on melamine tape or with wood veneer edging.

This is a very common style in Europe, as the name implies. Frameless cabinets are now popular in North America as well, because they are simple to build and often cost less than the face-frame style.

A typical frameless kitchen cabinet consists of two side boards, a top, a bottom and a back. Shelves and doors are all that are then needed to complete the cabinet. Usually, the cabinet is 5/8-inch-thick melamine particleboard with the exposed front edges covered with melamine tape.

Hardware Considerations

The North American traditional door hinge, which mounts on the front face of the cabinet, is difficult to install on frameless cabinets. That doesn't mean it definitely can't be used, but the 5/8-inch-thick front edge leaves little room for hinge placement.

Here is where the European hidden hinge comes into its own. It was designed for frameless cabinets, is easy to install and is the perfect companion for this style of cabinet.

All the overlay specifications have been developed based on the use of 16mm or 5/8-inch-thick cabinet materials.

Door openings, mounting plates and hardware fastening procedures are based on frameless cabinet styles. However, manufacturers have realized that the face-frame cabinet is still in demand and they have developed hardware to accommodate this style.

Doors and Hinges

You might think that the hardware determines the door style. Well, in almost all cases, that is not so. There are hundreds of hinge applications and, quite often, you will be able to mount any door style on any cabinet. It's simply a matter of knowing what is available and what the limitations are in some cases.

If the complex-looking European hidden hinge intimidates you, don't be alarmed. We all were hesitant when first faced with the need to use this hardware but, after the first few installations, we were amazed to find out how easy it is.

A typical "frameless" European cabinet.

Frameless cabinets provide the ideal application for the European hidden hinge.

Chapter 3   BUILDING DRAWERS & PULL-OUTS

TRADITIONAL STYLES

Throughout most of furniture history, drawers were made one way, and one way only. Two sides were joined to a front and backboard, and then an inset bottom was installed in grooves. The bottom of the drawer sides acted as runners, which ran on wooden tracks built into the cabinet.

I remember building many drawers, all that same style, and building frames inside the cabinet for the drawers. It wasn't a great system but it was the standard.

That inset-bottom tradition continues today among many cabinetmakers. Traditional building styles are sometimes hard to change, although most now use modern drawer-glide hardware.

The drawer face was either incorporated into the drawer as both the face and the front board or as a separately applied front. That choice was made by the cabinetmaker and was determined by the style of cabinet being built. Many cabinetmakers of long ago built very elegant and intricate drawers using all forms of joinery.

Cabinet drawers moved on wood runners before modern drawer hardware came onto the market.

MODERN DRAWER HARDWARE

Modern hardware now gives cabinetmakers the opportunity to vary drawer styles and construction methods. Side- and bottom-mount glides with three-quarter and full extension capabilities, along with positive stops and closing features, have opened a world of design opportunities.

Low-cost metal drawer glide sets that consist of two bottom-mount drawer runners and two cabinet tracks are quite simple to install. Installing the new drawer hardware demands special attention to the drawer's body width, as most of the hardware requires very precise clearances in order to operate properly. Otherwise, building high-quality drawers is well within the abilities of any woodworker or hobbyist.

Material Choices

In the past, it was common to use 1/2-inch-thick wood for building the body of the drawer. Today, all types and styles of solid woods and manufactured sheet goods are being used to build drawers.

Most common are cabinet-grade plywood and melamine-coated particle-core material.

Modern drawer hardware expands the design possibilities.

Cabinet-grade plywood, which has void-free layers, is a popular drawer-making choice today.

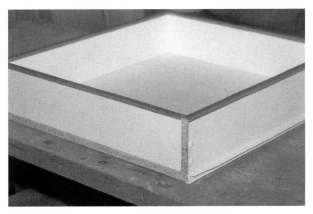

Melamine-coated particleboard is another popular drawer-building material. This one has a solid wood edge trim and bottom-mounted drawer glides.

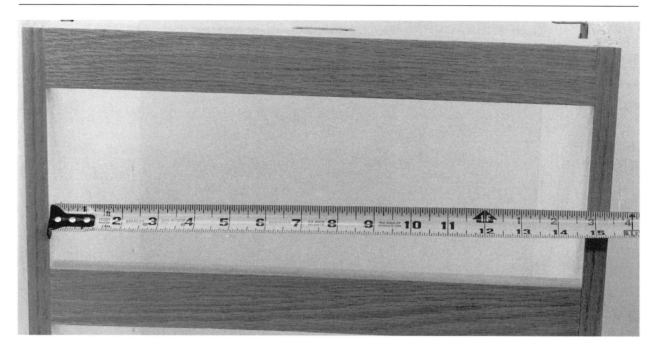

DRAWER JOINERY

Many of the joints discussed in Chapter 1 can be used to build drawer boxes. Rabbets, interlocking grooves and dovetail joints are still popular drawer-building choices. Butt joinery, using special screws for particleboard, is also very common.

Calculating Drawer Sizes

In general, the 1-inch rule applies to most drawer-building projects when using modern hardware. Bottom-mounted and side-mounted slides made by manufacturers such as Blum, Accuride and others, require a 1/2-inch space between the outside of the drawer box and the cabinet side for proper installation and operation.

The drawer opening is measured from inside the face frame, or cabinet sides if it is a frameless style cabinet. Subtract 1 inch from that dimension to get the outside width of the drawer box. To simplify

matters, I also subtract 1 inch from the height of the opening to determine my drawer-box height.

This "rule" is very general and I suggest you read the manufacturer's instructions that come with your hardware.

One important point should be kept in mind if you are planning to use the new hardware. Most drawer-glide systems are designed to operate with frameless cabinet building styles, where the cabinet is the same width all over. But that doesn't mean that the hardware cannot be used with face-frame-style cabinets.

If the inside width of the face frame is smaller than the inside width of the cabinet, cleats or spacers must be installed so that you can mount the glides flush with the inside of the face frame. It is a simple matter of attaching small strips of wood on which to mount the hardware.

Measure the inside width and height of the cabinet, and then subtract 1 inch from each dimension to determine the height of your drawer box.

BUILDING A TRADITIONAL-STYLE DRAWER

This drawer box is made of 3/4-inch-thick pine and has a 1/4-inch-thick bottom. This is the inset bottom style that has long been the standard.

For this example, the drawer box is 22 inches long and 12 inches wide by 6 inches high. This box is designed to have a false drawer front applied.

Materials List	
2 sides	@ 3/4" x 6" x 22"
1 front	@ 3/4" x 6" x 11"
1 back	@ 3/4" x 5-1/2" x 11"
1 bottom	@ 1/4" x 11" x 2 1-1/2"

Step 1-Cut two side boards. Each inside face will require a rabbet 1/4-inch deep by 3/4-inch wide on both ends of the board. Cut the rabbet with a dado blade on a table saw or with a router.

Step 2-The two side boards and the front board now require a 1/4-inch-wide by 1/4-inch-deep groove on the inside faces to receive the bottom board. The top edge of the groove is 1/2-inch above the bottom edge of each board.

Tip: Use a table saw to cut the grooves. Set the blade 1/32 inch deeper than 1/4 inch to allow for a little movement of the bottom board.

Step 3-The back is dimensioned as detailed in the materials list. No grooves or rabbets are required on this piece.

Step 4-The bottom can be any 1/4-inch-thick sheet material. I often use veneer plywood that matches the wood of the drawer box, but use of any good hardboard is also very common.

Step 5-Attach the sides to the front and back boards, using glue and finishing nails. The top edges of all the parts should be flush, and the bottom board grooves should line up on the front and side boards.

Step 6-Slide the bottom board into the grooves of the sides and front board. It should be flush with the outside face of the back board. Verify that the box is square, and then nail the bottom board to the edge of the back board.

Traditionally, when solid wood was used as a bottom, glue was not applied. Therefore, the wide bottom board could expand and contract. Today, however, ply and composite boards are used for the bottoms and wood movement isn't the problem it once was. Use nails only, or apply glue along with the nails. I still retain my old habits and I don't glue the bottom—but it can be done either way.

The traditional-style wood drawer can run on the extended side edges, or it can be fitted with drawer glides. Using drawer glides eliminates the need for wood tracks inside the cabinet.

Extended lower side edges can act as drawer runners if a track is built into the cabinet. If you are using this traditional method, some paste wax on the wood will help the drawer operate smoothly.

CABINET-GRADE PLYWOOD DRAWERS

A special type of plywood is frequently used to build cabinet drawers. It is called by many names, including cabinet plywood, Baltic birch and Russian birch.

It is special because the layers making up the sheet are "void-free," that is, they are guaranteed to be free from holes. This is important because it means that the edges of each cut will be smooth.

Many cabinetmakers leave the edges uncovered because sanding can produce a very smooth finish. The edges can be stained, or sealed with urethane or lacquer. The alternating light and dark layers making up the plywood produce a finished appearance.

The thickness most commonly used for drawers is 1/2 inch. Sheets can be purchased in a standard 4-foot by 5-foot size. However, you

Build traditional-style drawers using birch plywood.

may be surprised at the high cost of this material, so plan your cutting carefully.

The same process described under the heading "Building a Traditional-Style Drawer" is used when building birch plywood drawers.

Because cabinet-grade plywood is a composite board, drawer boxes are very stable and won't expand or contract like solid-wood drawers. It is also only 1/2 inch thick, so

you will gain a little extra interior drawer space.

Like solid wood, this plywood is nailed and glued in most cases. Either side- or bottom-mounted drawer runners are used for the tracking mechanism.

Next time you are in a furniture store, look at commercial-grade drawer boxes. You'll find that the majority are made from Baltic birch.

MELAMINE PARTICLEBOARD DRAWERS

MPB drawers are very popular in the kitchen cabinetmaking industry. Wood edge trim matching the cabinet wood can be added to the drawer edge as a finishing detail.

New hardware innovations like the bottom-mounted drawer glide have allowed woodworkers to use a wider range of drawer-making material. One of those products is melamine particleboard (MPB).

Drawers do not have to track on wood runners or on flimsy plastic glides. Cabinet-mounted tracks and drawer-box runners support the drawer box. The drawer material is no longer part of the track system.

Materials List

2 sides	@ 5/8" x 3-3/8" x 16"
1 front	@ 5/8" x 3-3/8" x 12 1/2"
1 back	@ 5/8" x 3-3/8" x 12 1/2"
1 bottom	@ 5/8" x 13-3/4" x 16"

Building an MPB Drawer

In this example, my drawer opening is 5 inches high by 14-3/4 inches wide in a 17-1/4-inch-deep cabinet, and it will have a false front attached.

Step 1-Calculate the size of drawer box you'll need. As discussed earlier, using Blum bottom-mounted glides, I make my box 1 inch narrower and 1 inch lower than the width and height of the opening.

Based on the size of the opening, my drawer box will be 4 inches high by 13-3/4 inches wide by 16 inches deep.

Step 2-Cut a length of MPB 3-3/8 inches wide by about 60 inches long. This material will be used for the sides, back and front

of the box. Apply edge tape to one long edge, and trim the tape. Cut the board to the required sizes. Taping first and crosscutting second will give clean, square edges on each end of the boards.

Tip: Metal drawer glides are available in standard sizes, so pick the closest size to your requirements. My drawer opening is 17-1/4 inches deep. A standard 18-inch drawer glide would be too long, so I have chosen the next size down—16 inches.

Step 3-Attach the sides to the front and back boards. Use two 2-inch screws at each corner. The screws must be MPB-rated (designed to join particleboard).

Step 4-Cut the bottom board accurately. Take extra care to make sure this board is square because it will be used to square the drawer box. Edge-tape the sides before installing, as they will be visible. Attach the back with 2-inch MPB screws on 6-inch centers.

Step 5-Attach the bottom-mount drawer glides to the box with 5/8-inch screws.

Here's a pointer: To achieve "chip-free" cuts with melamine-coated boards, use a blade specifically designed to cut this material, such as this MEL PRO blade by Tenryu.

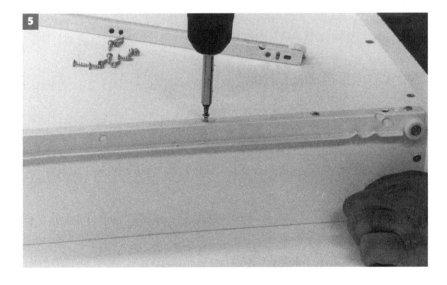

Step 6-Screwheads visible on the sides of the drawer box can be covered with plastic caps. If you plan to use these caps, drive the screw until the head is flush with the surface of the material.

Step 7-Use a carpenter's square to align the cabinet runners. They should be installed 1/4 inch above the rail, so position your square accordingly. Rest the leg of the square against the face of the cabinet, and the tongue on the cabinet side, then draw a line. This line will be 90 degrees to the cabinet face.

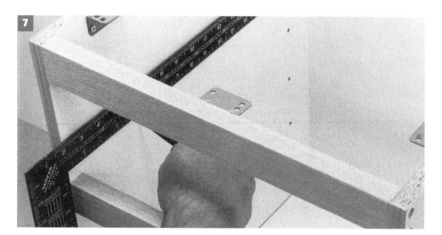

Step 8-Use the reference line as a guide to aligning the cabinet runners. Install one 5/8-inch screw at the front and one at the back of each runner, in case adjustments are required.

Step 9-Test-fit the drawer box and adjust the runners if required. Once you are satisfied that the drawer is operating properly, install the remaining screws. Finally, attach the drawer face of your choice.

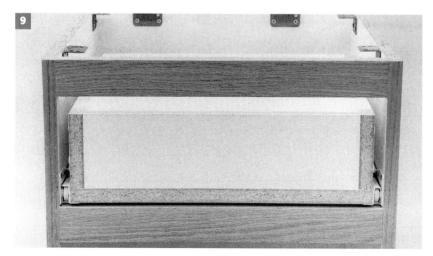

INSET CABINET DRAWERS

Inset drawers have their faces flush with the cabinet front. Building these drawers requires accurate cutting and assembly, as we are usually dealing with a 1/16-inch gap between the drawer face and the cabinet sides.

The following is an example of an inset drawer using the front board as the finished face. In this case, rabbets are cut into the front and rear faces, which is opposite to the process we used when building a traditional drawer with a false face applied. The front of the drawer will be visible, so we must cover the ends of the side boards.

I will also explain how to build these drawers with wooden side-runners. This is another style that was popular years ago, and some cabinetmakers continue to copy this process when building period furniture. When tracking the drawer on wood runners, waxing the wood is usually necessary to make the drawer operate smoothly.

Inset drawers are another style variation.

Building the Drawer

I will be using 3/4-inch solid wood for the sides, back and front. The bottom will be 1/4-inch-thick veneer plywood.

Step 1-Cut the drawer-front board, which will be the finished drawer face, 1/16-inch less than the drawer opening in height and width.

Next, cut a 3/4-inch-wide by 1/2-inch-deep rabbet on each inside end of the drawer face.

Step 2-The two sides are 1 inch shorter than the cabinet depth and the same height as the drawer-front board. Prepare these boards by forming a groove on the outside face of each side. The groove should be centered, and measure 3/4 inch wide by 1/2 inch deep.

Step 3-Cut a back board that is 1/2-inch lower than the front board and 1-1/2 inches narrower.

Step 4-Before the drawer is assembled, we need a groove on the front and side boards to receive the bottom board. Cut the groove 1/4 inch wide and 1/4 inch deep, with its top edge 1/2 inch up from the bottom edge of each board.

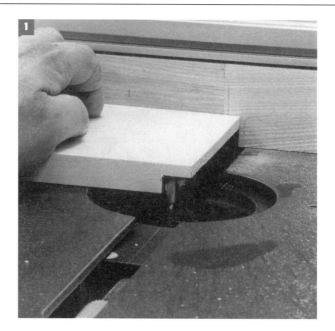

Tip: This can be a challenging drawer to build. Accuracy is important, so cut and position all the parts carefully.

The drawer rails should be smoothly sanded to about 1/64 inch less than the drawer opening all around, so the drawer will operate properly.

Step 5-Assemble the drawer parts, using glue and brad nails. Nail the side boards to the front through the sides to hide nail holes. The bottom board sits in the side and front board grooves and overlaps the edge of the back board as it does in the traditional drawer described earlier in this chapter.

Step 6-Cut two cabinet rails 1/2 inch wide by 3/4 inch high. The rails are secured 1/4 inch back from the face of the cabinet, which allows the face of the drawer to close flush with the cabinet face.

Position the rails accurately, based on measurements from the grooves on the drawer box. Be very careful when placing the rails, as their position determines the at-rest position of the drawer box. I recommend a 1/16-inch gap between the face of the drawer box and the cabinet face on the sides, top and bottom.

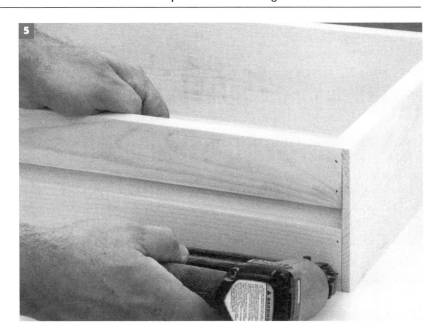

PULL-OUTS

Pull-outs are located behind cabinet doors and can be used for storage or for special applications such as shelves for CD players.

Two hardware improvements have made pull-outs possible—modern drawer glides and improved hinge technology. Cabinets no longer require a center stile because the new hidden hinges can maintain their position. Kitchen and utility base cabinets now have pull-outs routinely installed because of the mechanical ability of these hinges. But there is one item that must be considered when building pull-outs. Many cabinet doors enter the interior space of the cabinet when they are opened. Check the hinge you plan to use, because a spacer or cleat may have to be installed on the hinge side of the cabinet to provide clearance for the drawer glide.

Platform Pull-outs

The platform pull-out can be as simple as a sheet of 3/4-inch wood with a piece of decorative molding on the front. Or it can be a 3/4-inch-thick wood frame with a 1/4-inch-thick bottom. This is an ideal application for bottom-mounted drawer glides.

Pull-outs are "drawers" behind cabinet doors and can be any shape necessary to fit your requirements.

A wood-frame pull-out with a 1/4-inch-thick bottom, mounted on drawer glides.

Side-mounted full extension glides are also ideal for use with equipment pull-outs.

Making Drawer Pull-outs

Step 1-Construct a traditional-style drawer following the procedures covered earlier in this chapter. Remember, the drawer width may not be 1 inch narrower than the cabinet width if a cleat is needed to allow the drawer to clear the door hinge.

Step 2-Attach a false drawer-face as wide as the drawer box plus a little wider to cover the glide mechanism.

Step 3-Install the drawer glides. In this example, I am using full-extension side-mounted glides, but less expensive three-quarter extension units will work just as well

Design Notes

There are dozens of pull-out design possibilities. Large units in kitchen base cabinets improve storage; equipment pull-outs in the workshop save space; and entertainment-center storage of tapes, cassettes and CDs is much more efficient with a few pull-outs.

I use a number of tray and platform pull-outs in my workshop to store router and drill bits. Closing the cabinet doors helps keep the dust off my tools and the pull-outs allow me quick access to all my small tools. I'm sure you'll find many applications around your home and shop for these great storage devices.

Chapter 4   MAKING SLAB DOORS

WHEN TO USE SLAB DOORS

Slab, or flat, doors are made from sheet goods or from glued-up wood panels. They are a low-cost option to consider when a number of doors are required.

Utility and storage cabinets don't often require fancy doors, so the slab door is the answer. But don't sell it short—many kitchens, including my own, have veneer-covered particle-core doors, one of the most popular slab-style doors.

One 32-square-foot sheet of melamine or veneer-covered particleboard will yield quite a few doors. If you have a kitchen, bathroom, laundry or storage room project that you've postponed because you can't afford the cost of making solid-wood raised-panel doors, take another look at this low-cost solution.

Even the plain slab door can be made beautiful with a little imagination. Friends of mine tole-painted a lovely design on an oak-veneer particleboard door, and it looked great. This shows you what a little time and talent can do with inexpensive materials.

Tole-painting a design on veneer-covered particleboard is a great way to enhance the look of an inexpensive slab door.

MELAMINE SLAB DOORS

Melamine particleboard (MPB) doors are simply flat doors cut from 5/8-inch or 3/4-inch-thick melamine sheets. They are popular in Europe and are common here on low-cost frameless cabinets.

Step 1-Cut the door blank from a sheet of MPB. As mentioned earlier, this is where a dedicated melamine table saw blade is invaluable.

Step 2-Tape the edges of the door with iron-on veneer tape.

Step 3-Trim the tape with a double-edged trimmer. This trimmer is an inexpensive tool that saves time and does a great job of trimming the tape.

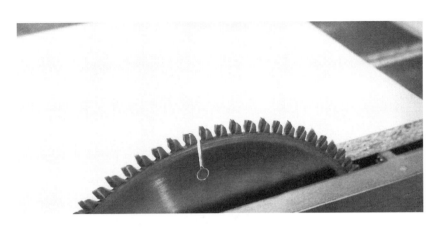

Tip: Even if you don't have a well-equipped table saw with a melamine blade, you can still make these doors. To cut MPB relatively chip-free with a circular saw, set the saw blade to a depth of 1/16 inch. Make an initial pass along the cut line to score the melamine coating. Next, set the blade to 3/4 inch deep, and complete your cut. If you have access to a router, make the first cut with a circular saw 1/8 inch greater than the required length. Then, using a straight-cutting carbide-tipped router blade, trim the board to the required size. The router will give you a perfect edge.

WOOD-VENEER DOORS

The steps involved in making this door are similar to those for the melamine door. However, we will be using veneer particleboard and wood-veneer tape.

Pre-glued, heat-sensitive wood veneer is available in all types and sizes to match any of the veneered sheet goods you choose. If you want a stronger door, you have the option of using veneer plywood material, but it is more expensive.

Step 1-Cut the door to size and apply wood-veneer edge tape.

Step 2-A double-edged trimmer tends to follow the grain and tear the wood veneer. I use a small router and a flush-trim bit to cut the veneer.

Step 3-To complete the door, clean the rough edges of the tape by sanding lightly, using fine-grain paper.

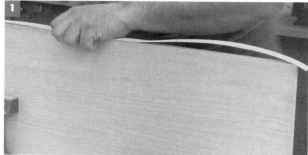

VENEER DOORS WITH A WOOD EDGE

Veneer doors are a great low-cost option, but it is impossible to rout an edge profile on these doors. However, the edges of a wood-edged veneer door can be treated with designs, which add a great deal of interest to an otherwise flat door.

Step 1-I will be using 1/4-inch-thick wood strips, so my door sheet will have to be cut 1/2 inch less in width and height from the door opening. Adding the wood edge will give me my required door size.

Step 2-Cut two hardwood strips 1/4 inch thick and as wide as the thickness of the door. They should equal the door width in length. Glue and nail the strips to the top and bottom edges of the door.

Step 3-Cut two hardwood strips 1/4 inch thick and as wide as the door thickness. They should equal the door height in length plus the thickness of the top and bottom wood edges. Glue and nail the strips to the sides of the door.

Step 4-Fill the nail holes with a wax stick that matches the final finish color.

Step 5-Using a router, round over the solid wood edge with a 1/4-inch round-over bit.

Design Notes

This door allows you to be creative without spending a fortune. Use a light-colored wood, such as birch, for the center panel and trim the door with a darker wood, such as walnut.

Varying the thickness of the wood edging permits the use of more complicated router designs on the door edge. You can use a cove bit or even a Roman ogee if you want a more intricate design.

This is one of my favorite low-cost door- and drawer-face styles. The wood edge provides a great deal of protection for the door. Most of the damage likely to be done to a door will usually occur on the edges. When it

happens to a solid-wood strip, such damage can be repaired.

I recently completed a bedroom set using this style on all the door and drawer faces. I spent about one-fifth the cost of solid wood and the bedroom set looked great.

VENEER DOORS WITH MOLDING

You can dramatically alter the look of a plain slab door by installing wood moldings. Make the molding yourself on a table saw with a special cutter, or purchase it at any lumberyard.

Design Notes

There are dozens of ready-made moldings available at your local lumberyard. Doors can be made to look big and solid by using wider moldings, while thin pieces will make the door look lighter.

You can also create some very interesting visual effects by finishing the door and molding differently. Using a dark stain for the door and a clear finish for the molding—or vice versa—can be very dramatic.

This door style also works well with plywood and moldings if you paint the door. It's a great look for the cottage or for those playroom cabinets. Blue doors with red molding will brighten up any child's room.

Step 1-Make a standard slab door with wood edging. Measure 1 inch in from all edges and draw guidelines.

Step 2-Cut the molding so the corners meet at 45 degrees inside the guidelines. Use glue and brad nails to secure the molding to the slab door.

SIMULATED FLAT-PANEL DOORS

Creating expensive-looking doors with relatively low-cost materials can be easily accomplished. Like the previously described door, this one has an edge molding that gives it visual depth.

Step 1-Cut a veneered particleboard door to the required size. Apply wood tape to the edges as previously described.

Step 2-The edge molding used here is commonly called doorstop molding. It can be purchased at any lumber store, or you can make it yourself with a round-over bit in your router. Measure the required lengths and cut the corners at 45 degrees. The flat edge is installed on the outside of the door and the rounded edge faces inward. Secure the molding with glue and brad nails.

Slab doors with mitered edge moldings have a flat-panel look.

Design Notes

This is another slab-style door that is inexpensive and easy to make. It can also be made from plywood and finger-jointed moldings if you are going to paint the door a solid color.

Doorstop molding is flat, so the depth is not great. However, you can create a more dramatic look by using a thicker molding.

This effect is perfect for cottage cabinets, in a utility room or on laundry cabinets. It adds an element of interest to the cabinet door without costing a great deal of money.

SOLID-WOOD SLAB DOORS

Edge-gluing boards will create solid-wood slabs that can be cut and routed for cabinet doors. It's a very old, traditional cabinetmaking technique that was popular many years ago.

Step 1-Edge-glue as many boards as required. A plate joiner makes the work easier, but be careful where you locate the biscuits.

Step 2-Cut the panel to size and round over the edges with a 1/4-inch router bit.

Step 3-A simple cross pattern on the door can enhance the look. There are many router bits available. Here I'm using a "V" bit to create the groove.

Solid wood doors offer many possibilities.

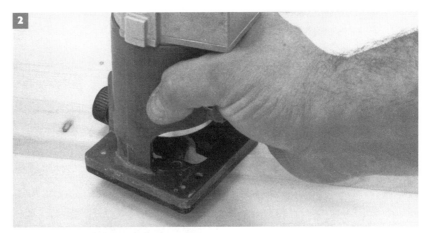

MEDIUM-DENSITY FIBERBOARD DOORS

MDF is compressed wood fiber that can be cut and routed easily. It is also used to make thermoplastic doors, which are growing in popularity.

The thermoplastic process can only be used commercially because of the very expensive and complicated machinery needed. Melamine-backed MDF, which is curved to counter the heat and stress of applying a plastic film, is cut on a computer-controlled router. The board is then wrapped with a plastic film, and heat, pressure and vacuum are applied to create the door.

However, you can use MDF sheets to make some great-looking doors. The board can be cut and routed easily. Edge and face patterns are quickly cut with various router bits.

MDF is usually a brown or tan color with a smooth surface. The color and surface texture result from extreme pressure applied when the wood pulp is compressed into sheets.

It is a very inexpensive material and can be painted or sprayed with solid colors. This board is the ideal material to use when you want to build a few new doors for your workshop cabinets.

MDF cuts easily, and all types of profiles can be created.

Melamine particleboard with edge tape make great low cost doors for those workshop or storage cabinets.

Slab veneer particleboard doors with an applied molding dress up any woodworking project.

Simple wood veneer particleboard sheets with wood edge tape look great and are an inexpensive door option for those large projects.

Chapter 5 FRAME-AND-FLAT-PANEL DOORS

FLAT-PANEL DOOR OPTIONS

Frame-and-panel doors can be loosely covered in two categories. The first are doors with a plywood veneer core panel and the second are those with solid-wood center panels.

Within each group are various styles of construction such as mortise-and-tenon, cope-and-stick, mitered and so on. But for our purposes, I'll classify them in these two broad groups and detail many of the styles.

Many woodworkers feel that frame-and-panel door-making is

difficult. However, just the opposite is true—it is an easy process.

As discussed earlier, the frame-and-panel door is made with two stiles, or vertical members; two rails, or horizontal frame members; and a center panel. The center panel can be plywood, solid wood or glass.

A problem that intimidates some people is the number of calculations and steps involved when making arched or cathedral-style doors. This, too, is a relatively easy process with straightforward measurements. There are a couple of simple rules to follow, but you'll soon become an expert at making these doors.

And finally, some so-called "rules" are really a matter of individual taste. I prefer to make my stiles and rails 2-1/4 inches wide. That's my choice. You might want to make yours 2 inches or 2-1/2 inches wide. It is not a major issue, just a matter of how you want your doors to look.

So don't be intimidated by the idea of making these doors. They are made with simple power tools and a few router bits, and can be quality-built by anyone in a shop of any size.

MITERED FRAME-AND-PANEL DOOR

The mitered frame-and-panel door is often used on furniture-style cabinets. The more common butt-joined style tends to be used on kitchen cabinetry.

I will be building a 14-inch wide by 24-inch high door using 3/4-inch stock. The center panel is 1/4-inch-thick veneer plywood.

Step 1-Cut two stiles that are 3/4 inch by 2-1/4 inches by 24-1/2 inches long, and two rails 3/4 inch by 2-1/4 inches by 14-1/2 inches long. Do not miter the parts yet.

Step 2-The stiles and rails each need a groove 1/4 inch wide by 1/2 inch deep on one edge. Center the groove on each edge. You can make this groove on a table saw or with a slot-cutting router bit.

Step 3-Next, cut a 45-degree miter at each end of the stiles and rails. The rails should be 14 inches long and the stiles should be 24 inches long. The groove on each board should be on the inside face, as shown.

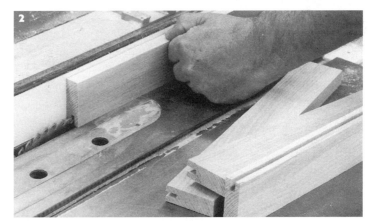

Step 4-Lay the door frame on a table and measure the inside dimension. Mine is 9-1/2 inches wide by 19-1/2 inches high. The panel should be cut to this dimension plus 1 inch on both the height and the width so that the panel will fit in the 1/2-inch-deep grooves.

Plywood panels do not expand and contract like solid wood, so cutting the panel 1/16 inch less on both dimensions is fine.

Step 5-Join two stiles to one rail using biscuit or dowel joinery.

Step 6-Slide the panel into the partial frame and make sure it is seated properly. Attach the remaining rail, and clamp until the glue sets.

Step 7-Once the glue has dried, sand the frame. Round over the outside profile with a 3/8-inch round-over bit in a router.

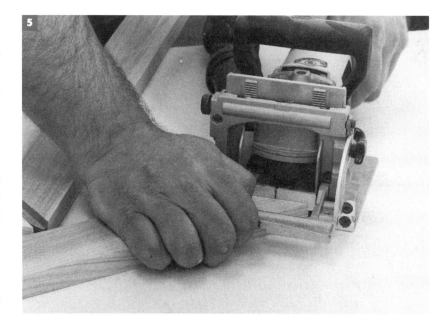

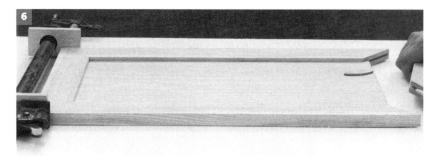

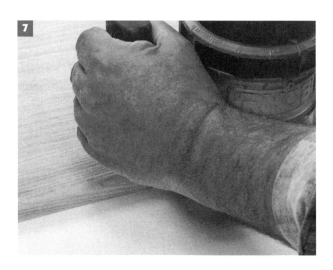

MORTISE-AND-TENON PANEL DOOR

The corner joinery on this door is a mortise-and-tenon, one of the most popular door-making joints. The joint is exposed on the top and bottom of the door frame. Therefore, a tight-fitting tenon is imperative.

This door will have a finished size of 14 inches wide and 24 inches high. The door frame is made from 3/4-inch-thick stock and the panel is 1/4-inch veneer plywood.

Step 1-Cut two stiles 2-1/4 inches wide by 24 inches long. The rails are 2-1/4 inches wide by 10-1/2 inches long. Rail length is equal to the total width of the door minus the width of two stiles, or 9-1/2 inches long. We have to add the length of two tenons, which are each 1/2 inch long, to the rail length.

The rail length formula is door width minus the width of two stiles plus the length of two tenons. As a further example, a door of the same style that is 20 inches wide would have 16-1/2-inch-long rails (20-4 1/2+1 = 16 1/2).

Step 2-Form a groove on the inside edge of each stile and rail 1/4 inch wide by 1/2 inch deep. Use a table saw or slot cutter bit and center the groove on each edge.

Step 3-Make a tenon on both ends of the two rails 1/4 inch thick by 1/2 inch long. Make certain the tenon is centered on the rail. These tenons are easily formed using a table saw.

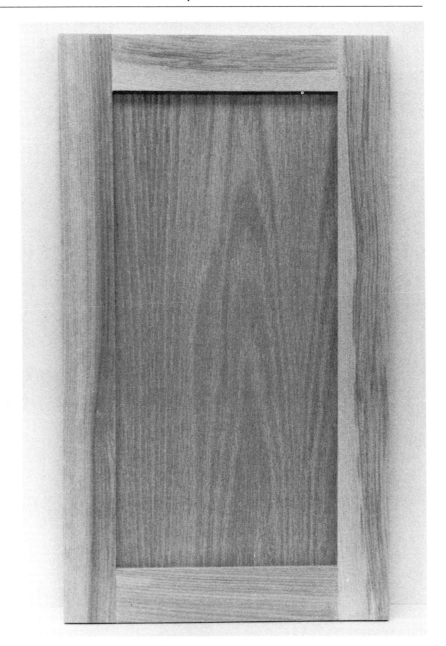

Tip: Cut the tenons slightly thicker than necessary. Test the fit by gently pushing the tenons into their mortises. Sand or file the tenons carefully until you achieve a snug fit. If you are doing a number of doors, have all the rails ready for tenon-cutting at the same time. Test the saw set up until you get a good fit, then cut all the rails. This procedure saves saw set up time and all the joints will be perfect.

Step 4-Dry-fit the frame and verify your overall measurements.

Step 5-Cut a 1/4-inch-thick veneer plywood panel that is the size of the inside frame dimension plus the depth of the grooves. The panel should be 10-1/2 inches wide by 20-1/2 inches high.

Step 6-Apply glue to the tenons of one rail, and clamp the two stiles to that rail.

Step 7-Slide the panel into the partial frame, making certain it is seated properly in all the grooves.

Step 8-Glue the final rail to the two stiles and clamp that joint. Use a square to check the door. If it has been racked during assembly, align it properly in the clamps. Once the glue sets, it will be held square.

Step 9-After the glue is completely dry, sand the door. Then it is ready to be finished. The outside profile can be left square or can be rounded over with a 3/8-inch round-over bit. If more detail is desired, you can use a fancier bit such as an ogee. However, always keep in mind the style and mounting requirements of the hinges you plan to use. If the outside profile of the door is too detailed, the hinge may not mount correctly. Test the profile treatment on a scrap piece of wood, then align one of your hinges to check its operation.

ARCHED FRAME-AND-PANEL DOOR

Cutting curves, arcs and other radius patterns in rails is a little harder than making a straight rail door. However, I think you'll find it's not too difficult to do if you follow these instructions.

This door has an arc cut into the top rail and therefore is referred to as an arched frame-and-panel door. I will also describe how the top rail can be cut to form a cathedral-style door.

In a kitchen, cupboard doors vary in width. The challenge is maintaining the visual appearance of all doors in the room, no matter what the width. To accomplish this, set the ends of each rail at a fixed width. I am using 3-1/4-inch-wide curved upper rails for this project.

The straight stiles and straight bottom rail are 2-1/4 inches wide in my design. So, to maintain the same look between a door 12 inch-

es wide and one 24 inches wide, I need a constant reference. I can achieve that look by making sure my arc is 2 1/4 inches down from the top center of all my curved rails-no matter what the door width. All my doors will have the same measurement above the arc, and only the radius of the arc will change. But all the doors, no matter how wide, will have the same reference above the arc.

The drawing illustrates the differences between rails for a 14-inch wide door and for a 24-inch wide door. Only the rail width and arc radius change, while all other values remain the same.

14″ Wide Door Rail

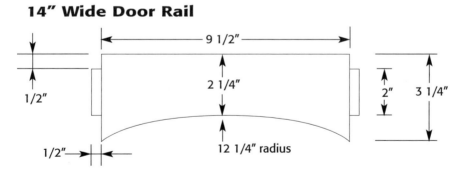

24″ Wide Door Rail

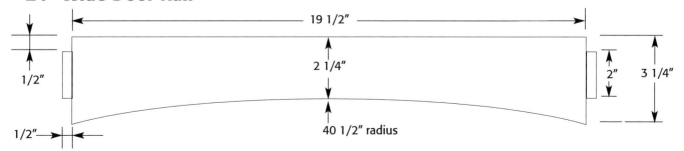

Building the Door

The door is 14 inches wide and 24 inches high. I've used 3/4-inch-thick stock for the stiles and rails, with a 1/4-inch-thick veneer plywood panel.

I have added another design feature with this door—the grooves in the stiles are stopped 1/2 inch short of the ends. That will give me a stopped mortise-and-tenon joint that won't be visible on the top and bottom of the door. For that reason, I have cut the tenon 1/2 inch from the outside edges of the top and bottom rail. However, the door can be made with a full tenon and groove so that the mortise-and-tenon will be visible. The choice is yours—either method is equally acceptable.

Step 1-Cut two stiles 3/4 inch by 2-1/4 inches by 24 inches long, and one upper rail 3/4 inch by 3-1/4 inches by 10-1/2 inches wide. The bottom rail is 3/4 inch by 2-1/4 inches by 10-1/2 inches wide. Note that the width of the upper and lower rails includes a 1/2-inch-long tenon on each end.

Step 2-Mark an arc on the wider upper rail, but remember to end the radius 1/2 inch short of each end. For this, I use an adjustable "yardstick compass," which is available at most woodworking stores. The arc should have a radius of 12-1/4 inches.

Step 3-Before cutting the top rail arc, form the tenons on both rails. Refer to the drawing for the top-rail tenon. The bottom-rail tenon is reduced in length by 1/2 inch on the outside to fit the stopped groove in each stile. All tenons are 1/4 inch thick by 1/2 inch wide, and centered on the rail ends.

Step 4-Cut the arc in the top rail using a band saw or jig saw. Leave the line visible when you cut, and smooth the curve with a drum sander.

Step 5-The grooves on the stiles should be slightly deeper than 1/2 inch and should be 1/4 inch wide. Because of the arc in the top rail, I've used a wing , or slot, cutter in my router table to complete all the grooves. The stile grooves should be stopped 1/2 inch before each end for a stopped mortise-and-tenon joint.

Step 6-The 1/4-inch plywood center panel should be cut before beginning assembly of the door. The simplest way to determine the correct panel size is to dry-fit the door frame and lay it on a panel. Lightly trace the inside profile of your door, and cut the panel 1/2 inch outside the lines. Using the frame as a template ensures a perfect fit every time.

Step 7-Assemble the door. If you are building the stopped mortise-and-tenon version, the frame and center panel will have to be assembled at the same time. Dry-fit all the parts together before committing to final assembly.

Variations of the Arched Door

Double-arched doors can be made using two wide rails. Prepare two identical rails and install one on the top and one on the bottom of the door.

As I mentioned earlier, a stile and rail width of 2-1/4 inches is my own preference. Some woodworkers like wider frame pieces. You can also make the arched top rail 3-1/2 inches or 3-3/4 inches for a more dramatic curve. It's a matter of personal taste, and I suggest that you use some scrap wood and experiment with different widths to get a style that suits you. Keep one rule in mind when building arched doors: Keep the rail height above the arc—at the center of the rail—equal to the width of your straight stiles and rails. If you maintain that dimension, all the doors on your project will look like a set, no matter what their width.

CATHEDRAL FRAME-AND-PANEL DOORS

The cathedral-style frame-and-panel door is simply a variation of the arched frame-and-panel. All the construction steps are identical except for the design of the curved top rail.

Prepare the stock as described for the arched door style, and cut the upper rail as shown in the drawing. This door can be made with either a through or a blind mortise-and-tenon joint. Both methods are common and are perfectly acceptable.

With my design, dimension A, which is the width of the straight run at the ends of the rail, is one half of the stile width. The material above the arc, dimension B, on the upper rail, also equals the stile width.

The arc radius can be changed by altering the width of A, but keep B equal to the stile width so that the door will look balanced.

This is my design preference—you may like another style. It's up to you. Try a few different styles with some scrap wood based on the formulas provided.

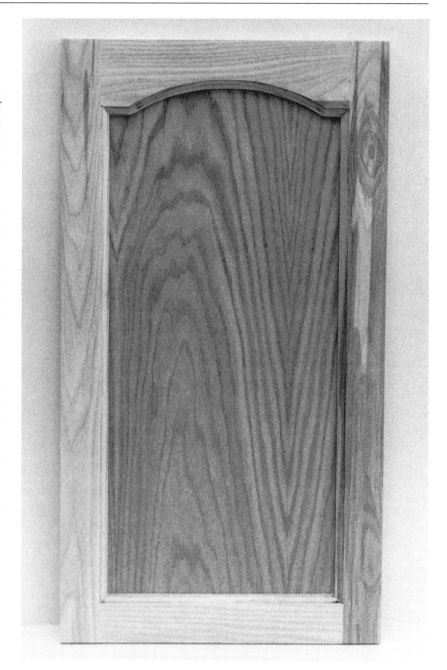

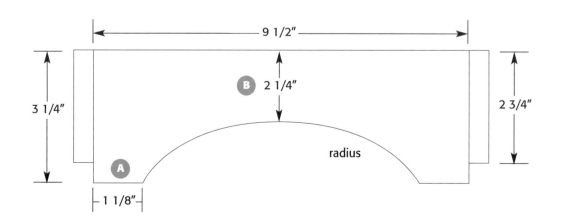

COPE-AND-STICK DOORS

Cope-and-stick is a popular joinery method that uses special router bits to cut profiles in the stiles and rails of a frame door.

The bit sets consist of a cope bit and a stick bit. Some companies offer a combination bit that will cut both profiles when the blades are rearranged, but I prefer the two-bit set. A third bit, called a panel-raising bit, is necessary when you are making raised-panel doors.

The stick bit cuts a mortise on the inside edge of each frame member. It also profiles a decorative pattern. The cope bit is used to cut a mirror-image profile of that pattern as well as a tenon on the ends of each rail.

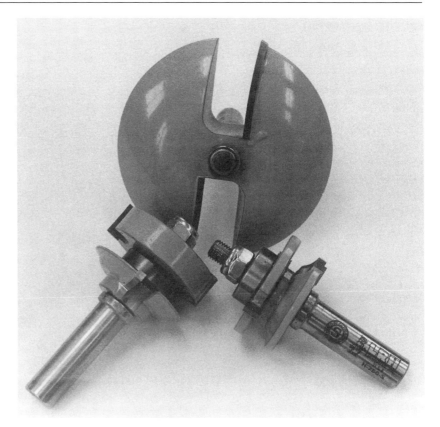

These are expensive bit sets, but are well worth the money if you plan to make your own doors. A good bit set will produce a high-quality joint, so be sure to look for well-made carbide sets.

Each cope-and-stick bit set cuts a little differently. Final door width depends upon the amount of material removed by the bits. For example, I tested my set and determined that my rail width, after cutting the stile and rail profiles, needed to be cut 3-3/8 inches shorter than my desired final door width. That is based on building the door with 2-1/4-inch wide stiles. So if I needed a 16-inch-wide door, I would cut my rails 12-5/8 inches wide. That measurement, plus 3-3/8 inches on either side, would give me a finished door width of 16 inches.

Test your own bit set and determine a rough-cut width for the rails. You should be able to determine the characteristics of the set you are using, and then produce doors of any width you need.

Cope-and-stick bits cut joint profiles in stiles and rails when you build this popular door style.

SQUARE COPE-AND-STICK PANEL DOORS

I've made this door using the cope-and-stick bit set with a 1/4-inch-thick veneer plywood center panel. The bit set will cut a 1/4-inch groove in the stiles and rails so the stock veneer boards fit perfectly.

The stiles and rails are 3/4 inch thick. All dimensions given are based on a finished door 15-3/8 inches wide by 28 inches high.

Step 1-Cut two stiles 2 1/4 inches wide by 28 inches long, and two rails 2-1/4 inches wide by 12 inches long.

Step 2-Profile the inside edge of each stile and rail with the "stick" bit.

Step 3-The cope bit is used to profile both ends of the two rails. Align the cope bit using a previously cut stick profile. Test the cut and fit with a scrap piece of 3/4-inch-thick wood.

Step 4-The 1/4-inch-thick veneer plywood panel is 3/4 inch wider and 3/4 inch longer than the inside dimension of the door frame. My bit set cuts a groove just slightly deeper than 3/8 inch, so I need a panel 11-3/4 inches wide by 24-1/8 inches long.

Step 5-Attach the stiles to one rail. Use glue and clamp in place, or "pin" the joint with a brad nail on the rear face of the door.

Step 6-Install the remaining rail after inserting the center panel. It is not necessary to glue the panel in place. Testing the corners with a square will correctly align the door. Set the frame correctly in the clamps if necessary.

Important Safety Advice

The pictures in this book show equipment operating without guards. That is for photographic clarity only and is not the way I normally operate my equipment. Cope-and-stick bit sets can be very dangerous because they are cutting a great deal of material. Make multiple passes instead of one large pass, and be very careful. These bits can do a great deal of damage to your hands in a split second. Use all the recommended safety equipment and procedures.

Cope-and-Stick Bit Sets

Not every bit set is equal in quality. There are some very good and some very bad router-bit sets, so it pays to do a little research when investing in these cutters. With proper care, a high-quality set will last many years.

Aside from quality, there are a number of styles available for your consideration. Complicated pattern profiles can dramatically change the look of your project. There are a few ornately styled "old world" cutters and a couple of more modern, simple patterns. Ask the dealer for the profile diagrams of the cutters, then choose the one that suits your taste.

For example, the CO-ST router bits from LRH Enterprises Inc., which I use, offer four very different cutter profiles with matching raised-panel bits. It is also worth taking the time to match the raised-panel cutter profile to the bit set you buy.

CATHEDRAL COPE-AND-STICK PANEL DOORS

Arched or cathedral cope-and-stick doors are made in the same way as the square door. The only difference is in the curved rail (or rails), which determines the style.

This cathedral door will be made from 3/4-inch stock and has a 1/4-inch-thick veneer plywood panel. The door is 15-3/8 inches wide by 28 inches high.

Step 1-Prepare two stiles 2-1/4 inches wide by 28 inches long.

Step 2-Cut a bottom rail 2-1/4 inches wide by 12 inches long.

Step 3-The top rail is 3-1/2 inches wide by 12 inches long and requires an arc cut as shown previously in the drawing on page 66.

Step 4-Cut the arc outside the layout line, and sand smooth to the line using a drum sander.

Design Notes

I have changed a few dimensions to show the flexibility of the design. My upper rail height is 3-1/2 inches, and dimension A (drawing, page 66), will be 1-1/2 inches. However, I maintain dimension B at 2-1/4 inches, equal to my rail width.

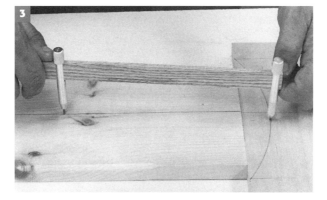

Step 5-Cut the stick sides of the joints on the inside face of each stile and rail.

Step 6-Cut both ends of the two rails with the cope bit.

Step 7-Assemble the frame dry and lay it over a piece of 1/4-inch plywood veneer. Trace the inside profile for your panel and add 3/8 inch. That is the cut line for your panel.

Step 8-Assemble the door, making sure it is square. Use glue at all the frame joints, and leave the panel free to move. Clamp the door, and sand after the glue has set.

Variations

A very nice mitered door can easily be made using the stick bit only. Cut the stiles and rails about 1/2 inch longer than the final door height and width. Cut one inside face of each piece with the stick bit. Do not cope the rail ends.

Next, cut the rails and stiles at 45 degrees. If I needed a door 14 inches wide by 28 inches high, I would cut my rails at 14 inches and my stiles at 28 inches.

Joining 45-degree corners can be difficult. I suggest you use biscuits or dowels, then glue and clamp.

A mitered door can easily be made with the stick bit.

SIMPLE MITERED PANEL DOORS

A simple but elegant mitered panel door, which appears raised, can easily be made using 3/4-inch stock and 1/2-inch plywood or particleboard veneer sheets.

I will be using 3/4-inch-thick hardwood for the frame and 1/2-inch-thick veneer particleboard for the center panel.

Step 1-Cut the stiles and rails 1/2 inch longer than the height and the width of your door. I am using 2-inch wide boards.

Step 2-Round over the front inside and outside edges of each piece with a 3/8-inch round-over bit.

Step 3-Next, cut a rabbet on one edge of each stile and rail, opposite the round-over faces. The rabbet is 1/2 inch deep and 3/4 inch wide. Cut the rabbet in three or four passes with a dado blade on your table saw, or on a router table. This is a great deal of material to remove and you want to avoid tearing the 1/4-inch-thick edge of the board by attempting to do it in one pass.

Step 4-Now cut the stiles and rails with 45-degree angles at each end. Their lengths depend upon the door size required. For example, if I needed a 16-inch-wide by 28-inch-high door, I would cut two 16-inch rails and two 28-inch stiles. These measurements are taken at the longest point of the miter cuts.

Step 5-Assemble the frame, with glue and biscuits or dowels. It is also possible to use small finishing nails at each corner if you don't have access to other joinery methods.

Step 6-Lay the door frame face down, and measure the size of the panel required. The size will depend upon your stile and rail widths, as well as on the depth of the rabbet cut.

Step 7-Cut the panel, then test-fit. Run a bead of glue in the rabbet and install the panel. It can be secured, until the glue dries, with a few brad nails angled into the frame pieces.

This is a cross-section of the center panel in the door frame.

Construction Notes

This is one of my favorite styles to use when I'm making high doors. The 1/2-inch-thick center panel stiffens and strengthens the door and makes this one of the best designs for pantry or closet cabinet applications.

I build this door often. I recently completed a project that called for 84-inch pantry doors. Standard frame-and-panel doors would require multiple panels to reach that height. I needed a door style that combined strength with the ability to remain straight. This particular frame-and-panel design was ideal. It is a strong door that doesn't cost a great deal of money to build when you compare it with the cost of materials for raised-panel doors. And, best of all, it looks great. Not only is there visual depth, there is also a soft look because of the rounded-over edges on the frame.

If you have a project that requires a large door, this is the answer—it offers good looks, is simple to make and is not all that expensive.

Chapter 6   FRAME-AND-RAISED-PANEL DOORS

SOLID-WOOD CONSTRUCTION

Raised-panel doors are made following the same steps we used for flat-panel doors. However, the center panel of the door is where these two door styles differ. As the names suggest, the flat panel uses a plywood-core veneer center, and the raised panel is made from solid wood with machined edges so it will fit in the door-frame grooves.

Raising solid-wood glued-up boards to form raised panels is not a difficult process, but it can be dangerous, so be sure to make many small passes and observe all safety precautions. That rule applies to all woodworking, of course, but is worth stating again here because of the large amounts of wood removed when raising panels. Many small passes through a router are safer, and further benefit will be seen in the cleaner, more uniform cuts.

Panel-to-frame Relationship

Flat-panel doors have 1/4-inch plywood center panels, so they are always lower than the surface of the frame.

Raised-panel doors use solid wood panels with milled edges. The panel face can be lower than or on the same plane as the frame facing. You can control the panel position by deciding on the thickness of the frame and panel before starting to build the door.

To make a door with the top surface of the raised panel on the same level as the frame members, use 3/4-inch-thick frame boards with a 9/16-inch-thick panel that fits in a groove cut 3/16 inch in from the back face of the frame members. Or you can use a combination of 7/8-inch frame pieces with a 5/8-inch panel set 1/4 inch in from the back face of the frame members.

If you want the panel face raised above the front faces of the frame-members, use frame and panel pieces that are the same thickness. This is a style choice you can decide on after you've made a few sample doors.

Panel Profiles

There are as many panel-raising profile bits as there are stile- and rail-cutter profiles. They are named ogee, bevel and radius, or cove, plus a few others by different manufacturers. However, most cope-and-stick bit sets have a matching panel-raising bit. Again, it's a style choice—one is no better than any of the others. Choose the style that suits you best.

Panel Material

The panels for these raised-panel doors are usually made by edge-gluing a number of solid boards. They can be attached with glue or with a combination of biscuits and glue. Both methods are commonly used but biscuit joinery is becoming more popular.

In some cases, the panel can be one wide board, but be careful, because

Panel-face to frame-face alignment depends upon the panel thickness.

a single solid board tends to cup and warp more than a number of glued-up boards. Twisting door panels can quickly throw everything out of alignment. So wherever possible, use a number of boards with growth-pattern rings opposing each other, to make your panels.

Panel Raising

There are a couple of ways to raise a panel. One is on the table saw, and the other is with a panel-raising bit in a router table. The router method is the most common, and different styles are possible, depending upon the bit used.

The first door we'll cover in this chapter is a raised-panel door made on a table saw. This process is a low-cost alternative to investing in router tables and bits.

Door Finishing

Raised panels will expand and contract to a greater degree than flat plywood panels. If you plan to stain the raised panel, do it before assembly, in order to avoid stain lines when the panel contracts.

Safety Note:

Remember these few words of caution before using panel-raising router bits: They can remove a great deal of material in one pass, but taking one pass is dangerous and isn't to your advantage because it will not produce good results.

Take many small passes, use high-quality bits with a 1/2-inch shaft, and take your time.

These bits must be used in a router table with a 1-1/2-horsepower router. In some cases, there is a motor-speed recommendation for these bits, so be sure to read and follow the specs on the manufacturer's data sheets carefully.

TABLE SAW FRAME-AND RAISED-PANEL DOOR

This door will be 24 inches high and 14 inches wide. I will be using 3/4-inch-thick material for the frame and the raised panel. In order to have a heavier-looking door, I've made my stiles and rails 2-1/2 inches wide.

Step 1-Cut two stiles 3/4 inch thick by 2-1/2 inches wide by 24 inches long and two rails 3/4 inch by 2-1/2 inches by 10 inches.

Find the rail size by subtracting the stile widths from the total door width (14-5 = 9) and by adding the two tenon lengths of 1/2 inch each to the rail length (9+1 = 10).

Step 2-Use the table saw to make a groove 1/4 inch wide by 1/2 inch deep on one edge of each rail and stile. Center the groove on each edge.

Step 3-The rails require a 1/4-inch-thick by 1/2-inch-long tenon centered on each end of both rails. Use the table saw and a regular blade to make the tenons. Make the shoulder-cut first, then nibble the waste material toward the end of each rail.

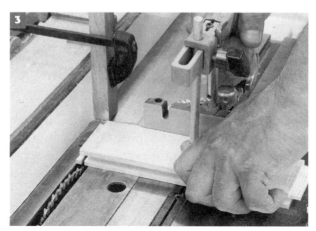

Step 4-The inside measurement of my frame is 9 inches wide by 19 inches high. My panel will be 9-7/8 inches by 19-7/8 inches so that it will fit in the grooves with a little room for movement.

Glue up 3/4-inch-thick boards a little wider and a little longer than required, then trim to a finished size. I am using biscuit joinery for my panel.

Step 5-Use the table saw to score the panel 1/8-inch deep, 2 inches in from each edge.

Step 6-Tip the saw blade 10 degrees away from the fence. I have extended the height of my fence to give me better control when cutting high panels. This fence extension is a nice feature and can easily be made with a few boards.

Set the fence to cut a 3/16-inch edge on the door. That will give the correct taper and the panel will sit in the frame grooves.

Step 7-Sand the raised section of your panel with a large, flat-sanding block. Assemble the door using glue on the tenon only—do not glue the panel.

Place small strips of foam in the grooves before inserting the panel to prevent rattling of the door.

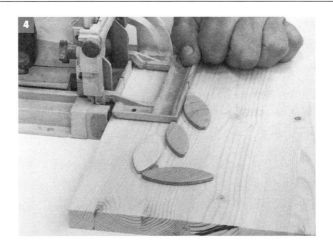

ARCHED AND CATHEDRAL FRAME-AND RAISED-PANEL DOORS

The process to follow when making an arched or cathedral raised panel door is the same as it is for flat panel doors. The frame is identical and only the panel-making procedure is different.

I am using 3/4-inch stock for the door frame and panel. The door size is 24 inches high by 14 inches wide.

Step 1-Cut two stiles 3/4 inch thick by 2-1/4 inches wide by 24 inches long. The bottom rail equals the door width less the width of two stiles, plus 1 inch for the two 1/2-inch long tenons. The bottom rail is 3/4 inch by 2-1/4 inches by 10-1/2 inches. The top rail is the same thickness and the same length but it is 3-1/4 inches wide, so that the arch or cathedral can be formed.

Step 2-Form a 1/4-inch-thick by 1/2-inch-long tenon on both ends of each rail.

Step 3-Cut the arch or cathedral curve in the top rail. Follow the procedures detailed in Chapter 5 for each pattern.

Step 4-Next, cut the 1/4-inch-wide by 1/2-inch-deep groove on the inside edge of both stiles and rails. Use a wing slot cutter on a router table. The curve on the top rail makes it necessary to use this router bit with a guide bearing.

Step 5-Glue up a solid-wood panel. Its rough size should be 1-1/2 inches wide, and longer than the inside dimensions of the door frame.

A 3/4-inch-thick panel will be 1/4 inch higher than the frame's face. If you want the face of the center panel flush with the face of the frame, use a 9/16-inch-thick panel and align the groove so that it is 3/16 inch above the back face of the frame.

Step 6-Dry-assemble the door frame and lay it on top of the center panel. Trace the pattern onto the panel face.

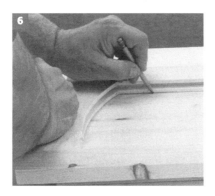

Step 7-Use the lines transferred to the panel as a guide. Enlarge the pattern by 7/16 inch on all edges. The grooves are 1/2 inch deep, so we must allow for a small amount of panel movement.

Step 8-Cut the panel using the enlarged pattern as a guide. A jig or band saw will easily cut the panel, but make sure the curve is smooth because the panel-raising follower-bearing will transfer any uneven curves to the raised panel.

It is a good practice to cut on the outside of your pattern lines and then sand to the lines. This ensures accurate sizes and smooth lines.

Step 9-I am using a panel-raising bit in a router table set up with a 1-1/2-horsepower router. The final height, or cut, with these bits should be set to leave a 1/4-inch-thick edge on the panel so that it will fit snugly into the frame grooves. Make a number of small passes with these bits until the edge is the desired thickness.

Step 10-Sand all the parts, then dry-assemble the door to test for a correct fit. Apply glue to the tenons only, and clamp. Check that the door is square, and set it aside to dry before finishing.

Safety Note:
Notice that I have a safety board on my router table. It is set at the center of my bit and wraps around the bit sides so that the panel cannot be drawn into, or past, the bit. Again, make a number of small passes until the desired edge thickness is achieved. Do not attempt to use one single pass. You will also find these bits make a great deal of noise, so be sure to wear hearing protection as well as your eye protection.

COPE-AND-STICK SQUARE RAISED-PANEL DOORS

This door will be 13 inches wide by 18 inches high. I am using 7/8-inch-thick stock for the frame and 5/8-inch-thick boards for the raised panel. My stick cut, or groove, will start 1/4 inch above the back face of my frame members. This relationship of frame to panel thickness will make the front face of my panel flush with the outside surface of my door frame.

As noted in Chapter 5, each set of cope-and-stick bits will cut a little differently. Test both the stick cut and the rail-end cope cut to determine the correct rail width for a particular size door. Once the dimensions are established for your particular set of bits, your door-width calculations are simple.

Step 1-Based on 2-1/4-inch-wide frame members, and my cope-and-stick bit set, I will need two stiles 7/8 inch thick by 2-1/4 inches wide by 18 inches long. My rails are 7/8inch by 2-1/4 inches by 9-5/8 inches.

Step 2-Cut the stick profiles on the inside edge of each stile and rail. Next, cut the cope on both ends of each rail.

Step 3-The 5/8-inch-thick panel is 9-7/8 inches wide by 14 7/8 inches high. It is cut to be 1/8 inch less than both dimensions, in order to leave 1/8 inch for panel movement. Raise the panel as previously described. Assemble the door with glue at the corners only. Check that the door is square, and clamp until dry.

COPE-AND-STICK RAISED ARCH AND CATHEDRAL DOORS

Curved cope-and-stick doors follow the same procedures as the square doors. The differences are the curved upper rail and the curved raised panel.

Step 1-Cut the stiles and rails to length, based on the final door size. Arched and cathedral doors require a top rail that is 1 inch higher than the straight bottom rail.

Step 2-Form the curved top as shown in Chapter 5.

Step 3-Cut the stick profile on one inside edge of all frame parts. Then cut the cope profile on both rail ends.

Step 4-Rough-cut the curved panel for either style. Next, use the simple trace method described earlier, taken from a dry-assembled frame. Add the groove depths, minus 1/8 inch for panel movement, to the traced lines and cut the panels. Raise them with a panel-raising bit in a router table following the procedures detailed in the previous chapter.

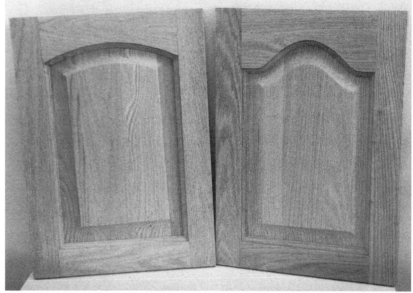

Step 5-Dry-fit the door. If all the parts fit correctly, apply glue to the cope-and-stick joint in each corner, but not to the panel. Check the door with a square and, if aligned properly, clamp until dry. Remember to pre-stain the center panel before assembly if the stain is darker than the wood. Staining after assembly may reveal clear wood as the panel contracts. Install a soft foam strip at the bottom of the grooves to stop any panel rattling. The foam will allow free movement and prevent noise caused by a loose center panel.

Tip: If you are going to make a number of doors that are the same size, cut a master template for the panel.

Chapter 7 MULTI-PANEL COPE-AND-STICK DOORS

These cope-and-stick panel doors can be made as flat or raised-panel doors. They are built like any other cope-and-stick doors but have cross rails and/or stiles to support the divided panels.

The cross rails support two panels and, because they are like a regular rail, must be coped on both ends to fit in the stick cut of either a stile or a rail. They must also be cut with a stick bit on both edges, because they nearly always support two panels.

It's not necessary to purchase additional bits in order to make these doors, because they are cut with the same bits that are used for single-panel doors.

These rails attach to any outside frame member, and are glued in place much like a regular rail.

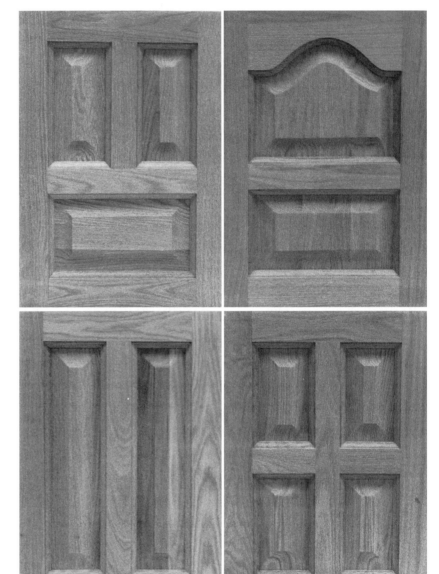

Cross rails have both edges cut with a stick bit, and both ends cut with a cope bit.

The design possibilities for multi-panel doors are endless. However, it can be a mathematical nightmare to calculate the panel sizes and curves. I suggest you dry-assemble the door frame and determine a rough size for each panel. Glue and assemble the panels, and place them under the dry-assembled door frame, to trace the inside dimension. Add the required 7/8 inch, depending on your bit profile, and cut the panels.

Then raise the panels with a panel-raising bit and verify the fit. Use foam in the grooves to help stabilize the panels.

If you plan to make a number of doors of the same size, create a panel template.

One step that will present a certain amount of difficulty when you make these doors is the sanding. Grain structures are often running in many directions, and the chance of scratching the wood because of cross-grain sanding is high.

I use a random orbital sander when sanding these doors because grain direction is not critical. Start with a coarse 80-grit paper, then sand the door with three finer papers until smooth.

Safety Note:
Be very careful when raising these panels, as they tend to be small and there is an increased danger when working close to the cutting tool. Use all the safety devices.

Cross rails are glued in place anywhere on the inside of the door frame.

Check multi-panel doors carefully before gluing.

Cross-grain sanding can be successfully accomplished with a random orbital sander.

Chapter 8   GLASS CABINET DOORS

ALLOWING FOR REPLACEMENT

Glass cabinet doors are popular in many applications. Kitchen cabinets, china cabinets, and display cabinets often use these doors.

They can be made in a number of ways but the common factor is the glass panel. Mortise-and-tenon as well as cope-and-stick-style doors are the most common types.

Once it was considered standard practice to build a door so that the glass could be replaced. Many, but not all, door makers are still using this method. In cases where special glass panels are used, a full groove is sometimes made to secure the glass. That is the style used for flat- or raised-panel doors. However, if the glass does need replacing, the door must be taken apart and it is often damaged, so I'll concentrate here on doors that will allow easy replacement of the glass.

Securing the Glass Panel

There are two common methods used to secure the glass panel. The first utilizes small moldings that are nailed in place behind the glass with brad nails. The second uses a commercially available rubber gasket. It may be difficult to locate this material in some areas. However, if you decide to use this method and the product is available, you will need to groove the stiles and rails very carefully to accept the rubber grips.

Commercial rubber gaskets are made for glass cabinet doors.

SQUARE MORTISE-AND-TENON GLASS DOORS

Building the Door

The glass cabinet door for this project is 3/4 inch thick by 14 inches wide by 24 inches high.

Step 1-Cut two stiles 3/4 inch thick by 2-1/4 inches wide by 24 inches long. The rail length equals the door width, less the stile widths, plus the tenon lengths—or 10-1/2 inches. We need two rails 3/4 inch by 2-1/4 inches by 10-1/2 inches.

Step 2-Each stile and rail requires a groove on one inside edge 1/4-inch wide and 1/2-inch deep. Center this groove on the edge.

Step 3-The rails are turned on one face and the saw fence is set to cut 1/2 inch in from the groove edge of both rails. Set the height of the saw blade to cut a little deeper than 1/4 inch. Cut the rails, forming a rabbet on the back side of each rail. Keep the small sticks that were formed when making the rabbet, as they will be used to secure the glass in the door frame.

Step 4-The stiles are cut in the same way, except that we will need to plunge them into the saw blade, leaving 1-1/2 inches of the groove uncut. Plunge-cut to start, and lift the stile off the blade 1-1/2 inches before the cut is finished. This leaves a 1-1/2-inch mortise at each end of the stile for the rail tenons.

Step 5-Finish the stopped rabbet by removing the strip of wood with a chisel or sharp knife.

Step 6-Before beginning assembly, form tenons on both ends of each rail, 1/4 inch thick by 1/2 inch long. Center the tenons on the rail ends.

Step 7-Assemble the door frame with glue in the mortise-and-tenon joint. I also secure the joint with two 5/8-inch brads. Make sure the door is square, and set aside to dry.

Step 8-Measure and order the glass. I use 1/8-inch (3mm) glass for most of my doors. Measure the width and height exactly, then subtract 1/16 inch from each dimension for easier installation.

Step 9-The wood strips that were saved earlier are now used to secure the glass. Use brad nails through the strips into the door frame. If you are uncomfortable nailing close to glass, you can purchase a manually operated brad-setter. It is not absolutely necessary to use the wood strips. Window-glazing or framing points will work very well on their own.

I often use a 3/8-inch round-over bit on the outside profile of this door. The door looks quite plain with clear glass, and the rounded profile helps to add a little interest.

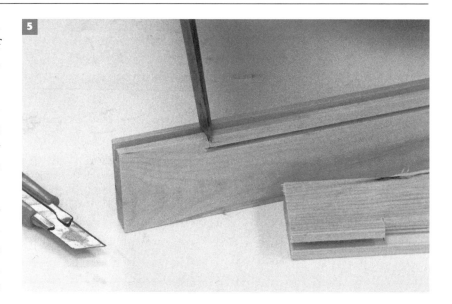

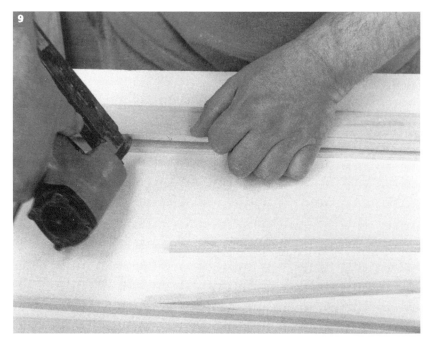

ARCHED MORTISE-AND-TENON GLASS DOORS

The arched door is made like the square glass door. The difference is an arched top rail. One variation on the arched or cathedral door is the use of curved top and bottom rails. The door size in this example is 3/4 inch thick by 14 inches wide by 24 inches high. Follow the steps for stile- and rail-cutting detailed for the square door, using only one 2-1/4 inch high rail.

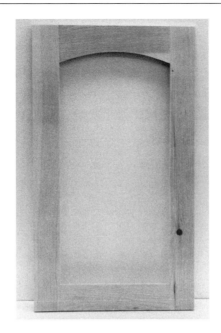

Making the Curved Top Rail

Step 1-The curved top rail is 3/4 inch thick by 3-1/4 inches high by 10-1/2 inches wide for a 14-inch door.

Step 2-Cut a 1/4-inch-deep groove on one edge of the rail. The width is 1-1/2 inches.

Step 3-Cut the back face of this groove 1-1/2 inches above the edge. That will form a rabbet 1/4 inch deep by 1-1/2 inches wide.

Step 4-Form the arch or cathedral top by following the procedures in Chapter 5 for either door style.

Step 5-Assemble the door with glue and brad nails.

Step 6-Measure the glass and install with wood strips or glazing points. Notice that we can use square glass by building the door with a deep rabbet on the curved rail. Using curved glass would be very expensive, so we want to avoid that situation.

COPE-AND-STICK GLASS DOORS

It is difficult to provide precise instructions for cope-and-stick glass doors. Each bit set is a little different and the process for cutting the rabbets in place of grooves varies with each manufacturer. For example, I can alter my set to cut glass-door frames by changing the back cutter on my stick bit. The manufacturer of my bits has provided a data sheet for this procedure. When you purchase your bit set, ask for details on this feature.

If the bits you use aren't adaptable for glass cope-and-stick frames, you can use the methods outlined for mortise-and-tenon frames.

Cutting the back side of the stick groove and stopping short of the ends on the stiles will allow you to install glass with wood molding or with glazing points.

Door Styles

There are three main styles of cope-and-stick glass-door frames. They are the open, the divided-light and the mullion frame.

All of these door frames are made using cope-and-stick bits that have been adapted for glass frames.

Most cope-and-stick bits can be altered to cut glass-door frames.

The back side of coped stiles can be cut to form a stopped rabbet joint for the glass.

Open Cope-and-Stick Glass Doors

This simple frame is fitted with a single sheet of glass. It is cut, as previously discussed, with a cope-and-stick bit set that has been adapted for glass center-panels.

Divided-Light Cope-and-Stick Doors

The divided-light door style uses full-thickness cross rails. Each divided section is fitted with a single pane of glass.

The cross rails are cut with a set of cope-and-stick bits suitable for glass doors, but both sides of the rail are cut with the stick bit. Therefore, each cross rail needs two cope and two stick cuts.

Both sides of the cross rails need a stick cut when panels of glass are used.

Mullion-Style Cope-and-Stick Doors

The mullion-style door has a full sheet of glass behind mullions that have been cut with a stick bit and reduced in thickness. It's meant to give the impression of a true divided window frame in your door.

The mullions are cut on both sides with the stick bit. I prefer cutting a full-thickness board equal to my door frame members. The ends must be cut with the cope bit before further cutting.

Once the full-thickness boards have been cut, reduce the thickness by cutting on a band or table saw.

Notice in the illustrations that the mullions are cut just below the curved bead section on the stick bit. The ends are coped so they will fit into an outside stile or rail as well as into another mullion.

The mullions rest on another frame member and are glued in position and fastened securely with clamps.

The width of these door mullions is a matter of personal choice. A door appears heavier with wider mullions and lighter when the mullions are thinner. Experiment with a few samples until you have a width that suits your cabinet style.

The mullions require stick cuts on both sides and cope cuts on each end.

Rough-cut a full-thickness board and reduce the thickness on a band or table saw.

This china cabinet illustrates the effectiveness and beauty of wood frame glass doors.

Chapter 9   **TONGUE-AND-GROOVE DOORS**

DOOR MEASUREMENTS

These doors are made of solid wood and are joined with mortise-and-tenon as well as with tongue-and-groove joints. There is a great deal of preparation required before assembly, but it can all be completed on a table saw.

If you only have to make one or two of these doors for a project, the calculations for the height of the center boards are quite straightforward. The challenge comes when you have a number of different sizes for a project, such as in a kitchen. When there are many different door heights, deciding which panel height to work with can sometimes be difficult.

This door style is simple to make and the door is strong. But do all the design and calculations before any cutting is attempted.

For example, I want to make 12 tongue-and-groove doors for a project. Three are 24 inches high, two are 18 inches high and the remainder are 26 inches high. A 3-inch-high center board will divide evenly into the 24-inch and 18-inch doors—eight for the 24-inch and six for the 18-inch. The 26-inch doors, however, cannot be divided equally by 3-inch center boards.

The best solution is to find a board height that will divide into all your doors. In this case, I would use a 2-inch-high center board for all the doors, but there are times when the door heights can't be commonly divided. When that happens, adjust the height of the center boards slightly to solve the problem. If one of those doors were 17 inches high, I would use a 2-1/8-inch center board. The extra 1/8-inch would not be obvious and I

would maintain a common look for all of the doors in that project.

Applications

The tongue-and-groove door is made of solid wood, offering both strength and stability. This door can be used for many applications. If you are building a project that requires tall doors, or wide doors, this style is an excellent choice. Since it has a "country" look, it is also extremely well-suited for country-style furniture.

This door can also be rounded over on the outside edge, or V-grooved along the stile-to-rail joint as I've done in this example.

Building the Door

The tongue-and-groove door here is 14 inches wide and 24 inches high. I have used all 3/4-inch stock but it can be made with material of any thickness.

Step 1-The two stiles are 2-1/4 inches wide by 24 inches long. Cut a groove on one edge of each stile 1/4 inch wide by 1/2 inch deep. Center the groove on each edge.

Step 2-This door will have eight 3-inch-high rails. Six of the rails will need a tongue-and-groove. The seventh, or top board, requires a groove and the bottom rail a tongue. The rails that need tongues must be wider. Cut seven rails 3-1/2 inches wide by 10-1/2 inches long, and one rail 3 inches wide by 10-1/2 inches long.

Step 3-Six of the 3-1/2-inch-wide rails, as well as the 3-inch wide rail, will need a 1/4-inch-wide by 1/2-inch-deep groove on one edge. Center the groove along each edge.

Step 4-Form a 1/4-inch-thick by 1/2-inch-long tongue on the uncut edge of the seven 3 1/2-inch rails. This tongue is centered on the edge.

Step 5-Both ends of the eight rails have a tenon 1/4 inch thick by 1/2 inch long. Cut the tenons on a table saw and center them on each end.

Step 6-Assemble the rails to the stiles using glue and clamps. Two of the rails have either a tenon or groove—these are the top and bottom rails.

Clamp the assembly, making sure the door is square. If it is racked, apply a little pressure on opposite corners to correct the alignment before the glue sets.

Step 7-Once the glue has cured, sand the door. A random orbital sander is the best tool for sanding in this situation, because of the cross-grain patterns where the rails meet the stiles.

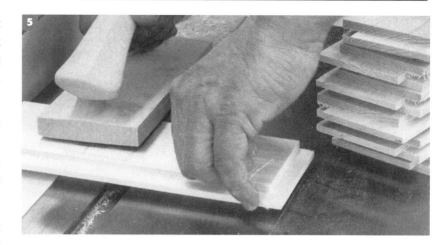

Step 8-There are a number of edge treatments for this door. I mentioned rounding-over the edge with a router bit, but you can also use any decorative bit that suits the project.

The rail-to-stile joint is sometimes difficult to align and close tightly. If there are even any slight differences in the rails, closing them all tightly is almost impossible. There may also be expansion and contraction at the rail-to-stile joint, causing gaps.

To visually enhance this joint, I use a V-groove bit and run a shallow cut along the joint line. I also use the same bit to ease the front edges of the door on all sides.

Chapter 10   MAKING TAMBOUR DOORS

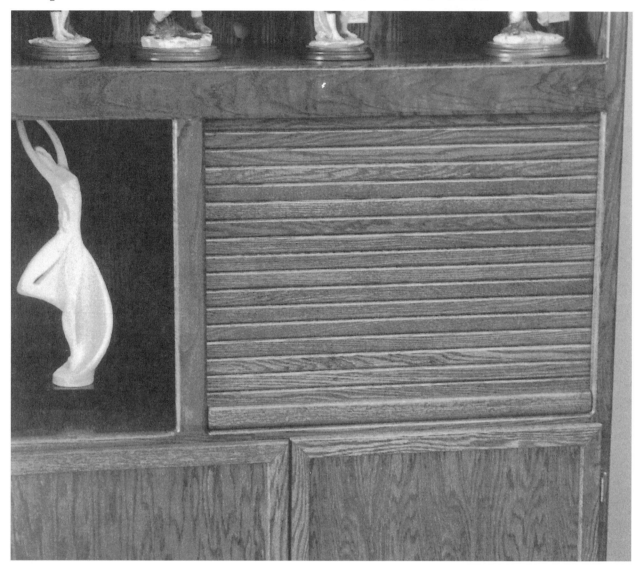

TAMBOUR APPLICATIONS

Building a tambour door might sound like a difficult process. However, just the opposite is true. It is a relatively easy, step-by-step procedure that anyone can accomplish.

Tambour doors have many applications. They are often associated with roll-top desks, but a "roll-top" kitchen storage cabinet—called an appliance garage—is frequently added to renovation projects.

The tambour door is also the ideal

solution for large cabinets that hold stereo equipment or for a home bar. It's particularly suited to a cabinet built to contain a television because, once opened, the door is hidden and doesn't block the view as a traditional swing door would. When you are finished watching television, you can pull the door down and hide the contents of the cabinet.

A tambour is made of thin, narrow strips of wood glued to a flexible backing. I have been using denim for the backing over the last few

years and I've found that it holds up very well.

Slat width and thickness are variable, but if you have an application for a small door with a tight turning-radius, keep the slats as narrow as possible. Large applications, such as the stereo cabinet shown above, can have wider slats because the depth of the cabinet provides plenty of room for a gently curved track.

There are a number of ways to build the door track. First I will be illustrating a router method using a straight bit and a template to cut a track into the cabinet side. But for cabinets with face frames that extend into the interior, a track can also be built behind the face frame. I will demonstrate both options in this chapter.

Building the Door

I will be making a tambour door for an opening 12 inches wide and 16 inches high. The tambour will be 13 inches wide by 18 inches high to fit into 1/2-inch-deep tracks routed into the cabinet sides.

Step 1-Cut a piece of denim 14 inches wide by 20 inches long. Mark the denim and cut it as square as possible.

Step 2-The denim is stretched and stapled to a board. The support board must be cut square because it will be used as a reference to align and trim the slats to length. Cut the board a little larger than the material. Pull the denim tight when stapling, but try not to stretch it beyond its normal length.

Step 3-For this demonstration, I'm using 5/16-inch-thick by 3/4-inch-wide by 14-inch-long pine slats.

Cut enough slats to cover the 18 inch finished height. In this case, I will need about 24 of them.

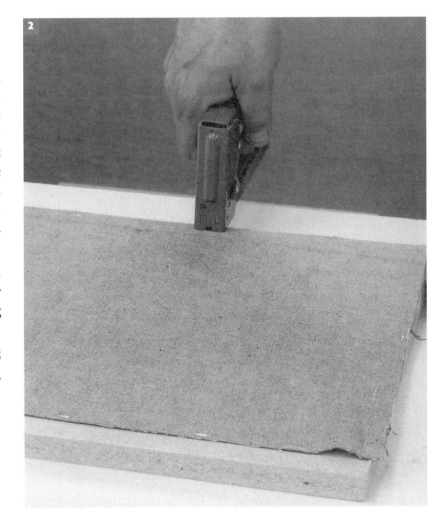

Step 4-Apply contact cement to the stretched denim and to the backs of all the slats.

Step 5-Once the contact cement is set, place the strips on the denim. It is important that the first slat is aligned at 90 degrees to the edge of the support board. Use a carpenter's square, and carefully attach the first slat.

Step 6-Place the remaining slats on the denim. Use the first slat as a guide and install the remainder tightly against each other as you progress up the door.

Step 7-The dry, or cure, time for contact cement varies from 10 minutes to half an hour, but I have found that it takes much longer to dry when used on cloth. The best way I've found to achieve a tight bond between the slats and the material, and not have the material buckle as it dries, is to apply weights to the support board. Turn the board over on a flat surface and place a few heavy objects evenly on the board. After drying overnight, the door will be flat and should be fully dried.

Step 8- After drying overnight, trim the tambour to its finished size on a table saw. Use the support board as a guide and cut through the door and the board.

Step 9-There are different handle options for tambour doors, including attaching a handle to the bottom slat. However, I prefer making the bottom stronger, so I often attach a 1x2 to the bottom slat, and use this as a handle. Round over all the edges and cut the 1x2 1/8 inch shorter than the finished opening on your cabinet.

Step 10-The track can be routed into each side of the cabinet. The distance from the bottom of one track to the bottom of the opposite track should be 1/8 inch greater than the tambour width. That provides a small amount of play in which the door can operate smoothly.

Cut a template and use a router with a straight bit and guide bushing to cut the grooves in each cabinet side. Run them parallel to the front edge of the cabinet until you reach the top rail. Start a gentle curve back into the cabinet.

The width of the track should be slightly larger than the combined thickness of the denim and the slats.

Step 11-If your cabinet has a face frame and it is inside the cabinet opening, build a track behind the face frame. The same curve and track-thickness guidelines apply.

Building a tambour door is relatively easy. Ther e are dozens of design options for the slats, so you should be able to make this door to suit any project you are building.

A heavy wood strip is attached to the bottom of the tambour. It forms the handle and strengthens the door.

Round over the support board and cut it 1/8 inch less than the width of the opening. Attach it with 1-inch screws through the tambour back.

A track can be built on cabinets with a face frame.

Tambour door slats can be cut in a number of different styles.

Chapter 11   INSTALLING POCKET DOORS

All of the door styles in this book can be used in pocket-door applications. In most cases, hidden hinges are attached to the door and ride on tracks. The door slides into the cabinet and, for that reason, pocket doors are always mounted as inset doors.

Pocket doors are a popular application for armoires and entertainment cabinets where a television will be installed. The swing door is not always practical for these cabinets because the door often blocks the screen. The pocket door system is also used where space is limited. You will often find this door in projects where an open door may block passageways or other cabinets. A bedroom armoire containing a television is a good example of this situation.

Pocket doors are inset, so it is important that your cabinet is square. The doors must also be accurately cut, as there is not much room for error. Take a little extra time when building the cabinet and doors to ensure a good fit.

I usually make my doors 1/8 inch smaller than the width and height of the opening. When the cabinet requires two doors, I make each of them 1/8 inch narrower than half the width. It will pay you to err on the safe side and make the doors 1/16 inch less so there is room for trimming if necessary.

Once the doors are installed, you can adjust them in three directions using the hidden hinges. Be sure to

follow the manufacturer's instructions to the letter when installing this hardware.

There are a number of manufacturers of pocket-door hardware. Each has its own installation procedures to follow, and most will provide detailed information.

I have used pocket-door hardware sets made by Julius Blum Inc., for a number of applications with excellent results. I have included the company's detailed installation procedures and specifications along with some special application information.

Retracting door hardware

· "Open and slide-in" door operation

· Epoxy-coated runners with permanently lubricated synthetic rollers

· Right- and left-hand sets with open channel design keeps dust from accumulating to keep action running smooth

· Adjustable two-piece steel follow strip

· CLIP door hinges and mounting plates that offer 3-way independent adjustment

· Vertical or horizontal installation possible

· Inset configurations for doors up to 19mm (¾") thick with included hardware or for doors up to 22mm (⅞") thick with optional hinges and mounting plates

· Runners, follow strips and plastic parts brown

· Hinges, mounting plates and screws nickel plated

Component list

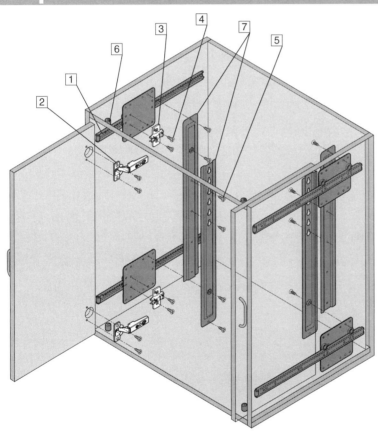

1 2 pcs. cabinet profiles (top and bottom) with pre-mounted guide roller and carriage plate. Left- or right-hand, brown epoxy coated.

2 2 pcs. 71M9680 CLIP thick door hinges.

3 2 pcs. 173H9100 CLIP mounting plates

4 4 pcs. 642.1150, flathead mounting plate screw (M5x11.5), nickel

5 6 pcs. 647.0700, panhead follow strip screw (M5x7), nickel

6 2 pcs. 270E0009 plastic door guide, brown

7 2 pcs. 270E5050 adustable follow strip, brown

Hinge assembly and adjustment

Assembly	Removal	Height adjustment	Side adjustment	Depth adjustment

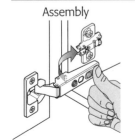   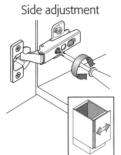 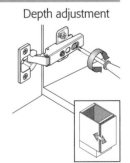

All measurements in mm   Courtesy Julius Blum Inc.

Installation dimensions

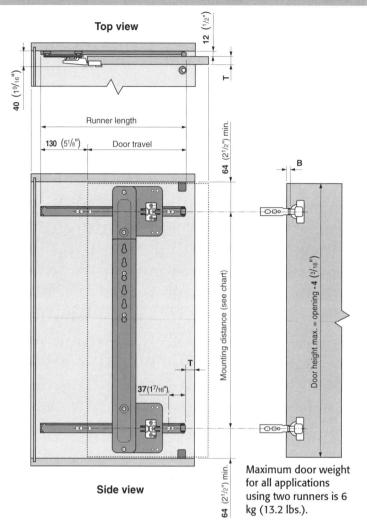

Top view

40 (1⁹/₁₆")

12 (¹/₂")

T

Runner length

130 (5¹/₈")   Door travel

64 (2¹/₂") min.

Mounting distance (see chart)

B

T

37 (1⁷/₁₆")

Door height max. = opening - 4 (³/₁₆")

Side view

64 (2¹/₂") min.

Maximum door weight for all applications using two runners is 6 kg (13.2 lbs.).

Inset applications

For 16mm (⅝") to 22mm (⅞") door thickness.

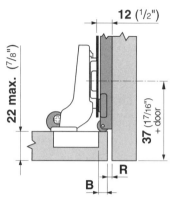

12 (¹/₂")

22 max. (⅞")

37 (1⁷/₁₆") + door

R

B

Reveal Table				
B Bore Distance	5	6	7	8
R Reveal	5.5	4.5	3.5	2.5

Reveal can be adjusted by ± 2mm

Mounting distance

Follow strip length	Mounting distance	Min. opening height
884 (34¹³/₁₆")	768 (30¼")	896 (35¼")
852 (33⁹/₁₆")	736 (29")	864 (34")
820 (32⁵/₁₆")	704 (27¹¹/₁₆")	832 (32¾")
788 (31")	672 (26⁷/₁₆")	800 (31½")
756 (29¾")	640 (25³/₁₆")	768 (30¼")
724 (28½")	608 (23¹⁵/₁₆")	736 (29")
692 (27¼")	576 (22¹¹/₁₆")	704 (27¹¹/₁₆")
660 (26")	544 (21⁷/₁₆")	672 (26⁷/₁₆")
628 (24¾")	512 (20³/₁₆")	640 (25³/₁₆")

Runner specifications

Inset applications:
 Runner length
 + Door thickness (T)
 = Min. int. cab. depth

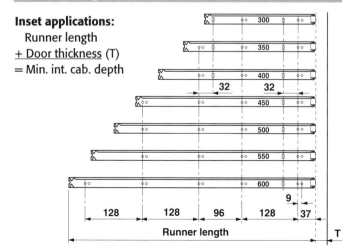

300
350
400
32   32
450
500
550
600
9
128   128   96   128   37
Runner length   T

Runner length	Door travel
300 (11¹³/₁₆")	170 (6¹¹/₁₆")
350 (13¾")	220 (8⅝")
400 (15¾")	270 (10⅝")
450 (17¹¹/₁₆")	320 (12⁹/₁₆")
500 (19¹¹/₁₆")	370 (14⁹/₁₆")
550 (21⅝")	420 (16½")
600 (23⅝")	470 (18½")

All measurements in mm   Courtesy Julius Blum Inc.

Vertical application

1. Assemble follow strip and attach to carriage plates with panhead machine screws.

2. Attach mounting plates (and spacers if applicable) to carriage plates with flathead machine screws.

3. Attach assembly to cabinet with 606N, 606P or system screws (purchased separately)

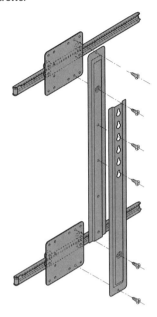
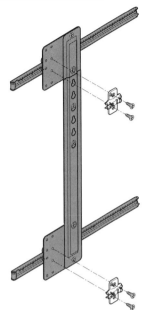
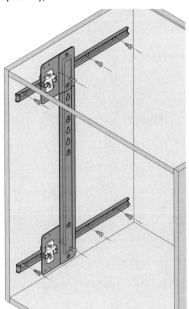

4. Attach door guides to top and bottom of cabinet with 606N or 606P screws.

5. Attach hinges to mounting plates.

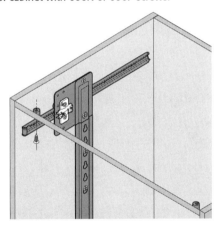
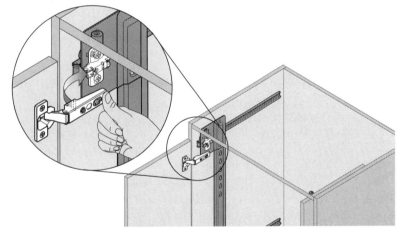

Horizontal application

Right or left-hand POCKET DOOR hardware sets can be used.

IMPORTANT!
Use FLIPPER DOOR rollers
Attach with 606N or 606P screws
(Purchased separately).

Max. door weight 6 kg (13.2lbs)

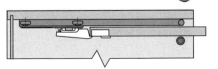

1. Attach assembly to cabinet top and rollers to cabinet sides.

2. Attach door.

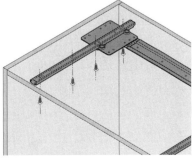
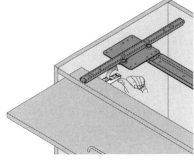

All measurements in mm   Courtesy Julius Blum Inc.

Alternative wood follow strip

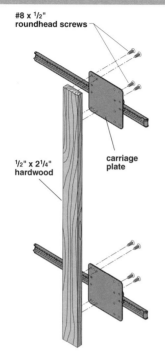

#8 x ½"
roundhead screws

carriage plate

½" x 2¼"
hardwood

Wood follow strip should be made of 2¼" wide x ½" thick hardwood and should be 12mm (½") shorter than interior height. Attach all carriage plates to follow strip with (4) #8 x ½" roundhead wood screws per plate.

Interior heights less than 640mm (25 3/16")

Side view

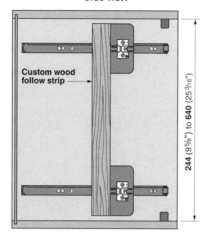

Custom wood follow strip

244 (9⅝") to 640 (25³⁄₁₆")

For applications where the interior height is too small for the two-piece follow strip to fit, a wood follow strip must be substituted. The smallest interior height that can be accommodated is 244mm (9⅝").

Tall or heavy doors

Side view

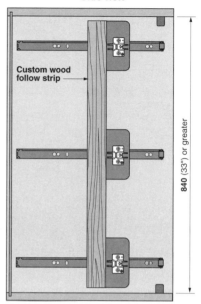

Custom wood follow strip

840 (33") or greater

For tall or heavy doors, additional hinges and runners may be required. When adding extra runners, a wood follow strip must be used in place of the furnished two-piece adjustable strip.

For frame cabinets

Top view

2 Hinge 71M9680
3 Mtg. plate 173H9100

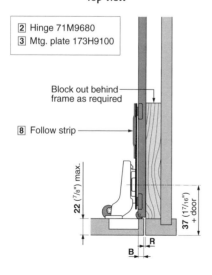

Block out behind frame as required

8 Follow strip

22 (⅞") max.

37 (1⁷⁄₁₆") + door

B   R

Use Inset application table on previous page

For frame cabinets with thick doors

Top view

Hinge 71M9780
Mtg. plate 173H9130
(Both purchased separately)

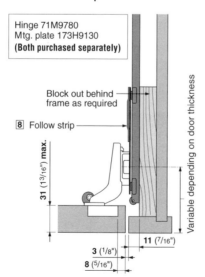

Block out behind frame as required

8 Follow strip

31 (1³⁄₁₆") max.

Variable depending on door thickness

11 (⁷⁄₁₆")

3 (⅛")
8 (⁵⁄₁₆")

For tall, short or heavy doors

Top view

2 Hinge 71M9680
3 Mtg. plate 173H9100

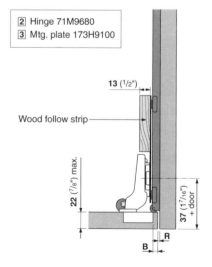

13 (½")

Wood follow strip

22 (⅞") max.

37 (1⁷⁄₁₆") + door

B   R

Use Inset application table on previous page

All measurements in mm   Courtesy Julius Blum Inc.

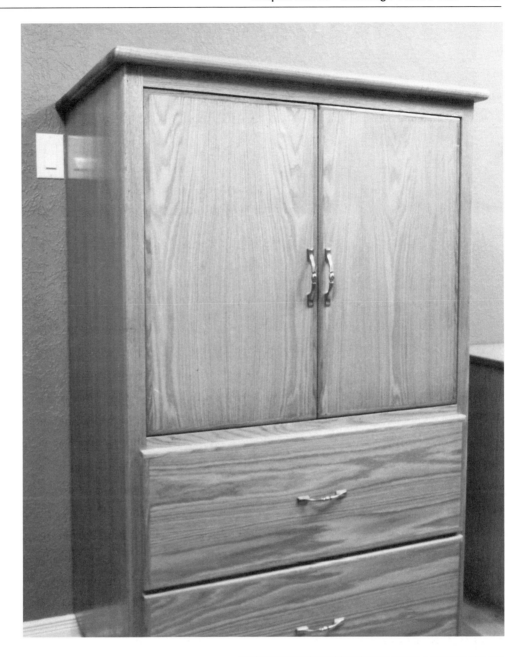

Pocket doors are the perfect solution for television armoire projects. When closed they hide all the electronic equipment.

In their fully open position, pocket doors allow everyone to see the television from any angle.

Chapter 12 INSTALLING DOORS & DRAWER FRONTS

SOLVING PROBLEMS

I've covered some of the following topics briefly earlier in this book. However, I would like to expand on my solutions to some problems that seem to bother quite a few woodworkers.

Custom Drawer and Door Sizes

If you are building a cabinet based on a plan you have purchased, it isn't absolutely necessary to know how to calculate door dimensions. But what if a standard 36-inch cabinet is too big for your space, and you need a 33-1/2-inch version instead?

Much is determined by the cabinet style. A frameless cabinet must be treated differently from a face-frame version. You must also know your door-closing styles in advance. Is this a full overlay door or an inset type? How much space is needed for drawer and door clearance? Does the cabinet have a center stile? Does it require two doors? These are some of the important questions.

Hinge Style

In Chapter 2, I discussed some of the door-hanging hardware available. It is divided into two basic groups—the hidden and the exposed hinge.

The traditional North American-style hinge is usually mounted on a face-frame-style cabinet. This style of hardware requires at least 1/2inch of mounting space beside the door for proper installation.

The European-style hidden hinge does not require any cabinet space beside the door because it is mounted on the inside of the cabinet.

Determining Door and Drawer Sizes

In general, door size is calculated by adding 1 inch to the height and width of the opening. For example, a cabinet with an opening 13 inches wide and 18 inches high will require a 14-inch by 19-inch door or drawer front.

If you are using a hidden hinge, the door size can be calculated, and the door mounted, using that formula. If it's a surface-mount traditional hinge, the face frame must be at least 1 inch wide to allow space for mounting the hinge.

Cabinets that do not have a center stile are best fitted with doors on hidden hinges, because these hinges hold their position and can be adjusted.

Drawer sizes fall into the same general category. Most drawer-fronts operate properly with a 1/2-inch overlay.

When the cabinet has a center stile, each section is treated as a separate opening. Add 1 inch to the height and width for each door. That formula will make each door overlay the center stile by 1/2 inch, so make certain the stile is 1-1/4 inches wide or wider.

The adjustable hidden hinge is an ideal choice for cabinets without a center stile.

Installing Drawer-fronts

It is not always possible to get inside the drawer box from above when attempting to attach drawer fronts. If you can't hold the drawer front in place during installation, here's an easy and reliable installation method:

Step 1-Before installing the drawer front, carefully drill holes for the handle.

Step 2-Place the drawer front in position on the cabinet with the drawer box in place. Install wood screws through the handle holes into the drawer box.

Step 3-Now that the drawer front is secure, pull out the assembly and install wood screws. Screws should be driven at least halfway into the thickness of the drawer front.

Step 4-Once the drawer front is secure, remove the screws from the handle holes and then install the handle.

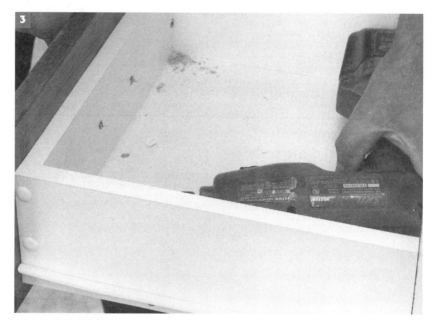

Installing the Hidden Hinge

Mounting and installing the European hidden hinge seems difficult to many woodworkers. It's one of the reasons why some people avoid using this hardware. Well, here is a simple installation procedure that works every time and does not require any special tools.

In Chapter 2, I discussed hinge types and briefly discussed installation procedures. The following procedure applies to hinges with an opening angle of 90 to 120 degrees.

Step 1-Drill the 35mm diameter holes in the door according to the data supplied with the hardware. Use a square to mount the hinges 90 degrees to the edge of the door.

Step 2-Install the mounting plate on the hinge body. I prefer using a clip-on mounting plate because it allows the door to be removed from the cabinet without disturbing any adjustments.

Step 3-Make a spacer 3/16 inch thick by 3/4 inch wide and as long as the door height. This is easily made from any scrap piece of lumber.

Step 4-Hold the door in the open position with the spacer between the door and the cabinet face. The door should also be held in its proper vertical position. Use two 5/8-inch screws to secure the hinge to the sides of the cabinet.

Step 5-Remove the door hinges from the mounting plates and install the remaining screws.

Step 6-Re-install the door to verify the alignment. Adjust the hinges if necessary.

Hinges for Glass Doors

There are hinges made for glass doors that do not require holes. They are designed to secure the plate glass with screws tightened on a metal plate. The plate is attached to the glass door with double-sided adhesive strips.

The handle hardware is also attached to the glass with adhesive gaskets. And this metal handle can be used as a door-latch that is held closed with a magnet.

Bi-fold Door Applications

Some cabinets, such as the kitchen corner base with a pie-cut Lazy Susan, require two doors, about 10 inches wide, hinged to each other.

The hinge can be a simple piano type that comes in long strips and is cut to the door height. The European version is a bi-fold hinge that needs a 35mm hole drilled in one of the doors.

If you plan to use the European hidden-hinge version, pay close attention to the hole position. Many of these hinges need the hole centered about 12.5mm from the door edge. That is much closer than a regular hidden hinge. In fact, the hole is drilled outside the door edge.

Sink Drawer-Fronts

If you plan to build a sink cabinet, consider one of the flip-out kits that convert a false drawer front into a useful space. These kits include the hinges and the trays and are very easy to install.

Glass doors can be installed with special hinges.

A metal handle is attached to the glass door with an adhesive pad, and the door is held closed with a magnetic catch.

The flip-out hinge kit is a great alternative to the false drawer front on a sink cabinet.

INDEX

A

Adhesives 11
     contact cement 98
Arcs   *marking* 64

B

Biscuit joiner *mini* 14
Biscuit joint 11, 12, 14, 55, 60, 77
Box (finger) joint 18, 54
Butt joint 11, 59

C

Cabinets *face-frame* 31-32, 36, 107
     frameless 31, 33, 36,107

D

Dado joint 15
     double 15
Door handles *choosing* 29
     mounting 29
Doors   *(see also Hinges)*
     anatomy of 22
     arched and cathedral
      frame-and-raised-panel 78
     arched frame-and-panel 63-65
     arched mortise-and-tenon glass..........87
     bi-fold 110
     cathedral cope-and-stick..............70-71
     cathedral frame-and-flat-panel............66
     cope-and-stick 16, 67
     cope-and-stick glass 88-90
     cope-and-stick raised arch
      and cathedral 81
     cope-and-stick square
      raised-panel.................................80
     design...22-33
     double-arched 65
     flat-panel design 54, 58
     frame-and-flat-panel............................58-73
     frame-and-raised panel 10, 74, 81
     glass 30, 84-91, 110
     inset 22
     joinery for 10-21
     mitered frame-and-panel.................59-60
     mortise-and-tenon panel 61-62
     mounting hardware for.....................23-28

     mullion-style cope-and stick glass 90
     multi-panel cope-and-stick...............82-83
     overlay..22
     pocket 100-105
     raised-panel 16, 74-81
     sanding cross-grain 83
     simple mitered panel 72-73
     sizing 30, 107
     slab 48-57
     slab, decorating...................................48
     slab, medium-density fiberboard 56
     slab, melamine 49
     slab, solid wood 55
     slab, with moldings 53, 54
     slab, wood veneer..............................50-53
     square cope-and-stick panel..........68-69
     square mortise-and-tenon glass 85-86
     tambour 96-99
     thermoplastic 30
     tongue-and-groove 92-95
     veneer 50-52, 53
Dovetail joint *cutting by hand* 20-21
     cutting with router 19
Dowels 11, 12
Drawers *fronts, installing*............................108
     hardware for 35, 36, 38, 40,42, 46
     inset...43-45
     joinery in 10-21, 36
     material for 35
     melamine particleboard 40-42
     plywood 39
     pull-out 46-47
     sink front 110
     sizing...36, 107
     styles of 34, 43, 46, 47
     traditional 37-38
     wood runners for 34, 40, 43

F

Fasteners *mechanical* 11, 41
Finger joint *(see Box Joint)*
Finishing *raised-panel doors* 75
Foam gaskets *for raised-panel doors* 77

G

Gaskets *for glass-panel doors* 84
Glass   *(See Doors, glass)*

H

Half-lap joint 15
Hinges   *European*..................23, 32, 33, 107, 109
                 flip-out..110
                 for face-frame cabinets 31-32
                 for frameless cabinets 33
                 for glass-panel doors 110
                 full overlay....................................26
                 half-overlay 27
                 inset..27
                 installing 24-28
                 mounting.................................24-25
                 North American 23, 32, 33, 107
                 parts of 23

J

Jigs   *box joint* 18
                 door-mounting..............................24
                 dovetail 19
                 tenoning 17
Joinery   *(see also specific joints)* 10-21
                 cope-and-stick 67
                 stresses in 10
                 wood movement in 10

M

Medium-density fiberboard 30, 56
Miter joint 14, 54, 59, 71
Moldings   *in door design* 53, 54
Mortise-and-tenon 17, 61, 85-86, 92-95
                 tenoning jig...................................17

P

Particleboard 11, 35
                 drilling 26
                 melamine-coated 40, 41, 49
                 screws for....................................11, 41
Plate joinery   *(see Biscuit Joinery)*
Plywood   *drilling* 26
                 for drawers 35, 39

R

Rabbet joint 15, 44, 72
Router   *box joint with* 18
                 cope-and-stick........67, 68-69, 80, 88, 90
                 dovetail with 19
                 panel-raising bits for 75
                 safety 9, 69, 74, 75, 79, 82, 83

S

Safety 8-9, 69, 74, 75, 79, 82, 83
                 equipment 8-9
Sanding   *cross-grain* 83
Screwhead caps..42
Screws   *particleboard*..............................11, 41
Sink drawer fronts...110
Spline joint 13

T

Table saw   *box joint with* 18
                 grooves with 37
                 melamine blade for.........................41, 49
                 mortise-and-tenon joint with 17, 85-86
                 raised panels with 75, 76-77
                 splining with 13
                 tongue-and-groove joint with ..16, 93-94
Tambour doors 96-99
Tongue-and-groove joint 16, 93-95

W

Wood   *movement*............................10, 38, 39, 60
                 orientation in panels 11

Text and photography: Danny Proulx
Produced by Cambium Associates, Inc.
Editorial: Kay L. Davies and Laura Tringali
Production: Bran Chapman and Morgan Kelsey